BIRDS AND BISON

BIRDS AND BISON

Poems by

CLAIRE MALROUX

Translated by

Marilyn Hacker

THE SHEEP MEADOW PRESS
RIVERDALE-ON-HUDSON, NEW YORK

All inquiries and permission requests should be addressed to:
The Sheep Meadow Press, P.O. Box 1345
Riverdale-on-Hudson, NY 10471

Designed and typeset by The Sheep Meadow Press.
Distributed by The University Press of New England.

Printed on acid-free paper in the United States. This book meets the guidelines for permanence and durability of the Committee on Production Guidelines for Book Longevity of the Council on Library Resources.

The Library of Congress Cataloging-in-Publication Data

Malroux, Claire.
   [Bisons et oiseaux. English & French]
   Birds and bison : poems / by Claire Malroux ; translated by Marilyn Hacker.
      p. cm.
   Poems in French with parallel English translation.
   ISBN 1-931357-25-0 (acid-free paper)
   I. Hacker, Marilyn, 1942- II. Title.
PQ2678.O88B5713 2004
841'.914--dc22
                                        2004011173
We are grateful to the New York State Council on the Arts, a state agency, for their support.

ALSO BY CLAIRE MALROUX

Les Orpailleurs, Rougerie, 1978
Au bord, Rougerie, 1981
Aires, Rougerie, 1985
Entre nous et la lumière, Rougerie, 1992
Edge, translated by Marilyn Hacker, Wake Forest University Press,
    1996
Soleil de jadis, *récit poeme*, preface by Alain Borer, Le Castor Astral,
    1998; translated by Marilyn Hacker under the title *A Long-Gone
    Sun*, Sheep Meadow Press, 2000
Reverdir, Rougerie, 2000
Suspens, Le Castor Astral, 2001
Ni si lointain, Le Castor Astral, 2004

ABOUT THE TRANSLATOR:

Marilyn Hacker has also translated *She Says* (Greywolf Press, June 2003) and *Here There Was Once a Country* (Oberlin College Press, May 1, 2001) by Venus Khoury-Ghata. Among the books of her own poetry that she has published are *Presentation Piece*, which was awarded the National Book Award; *Selected Poems : 1965-1990*, which received the Poet's Prize; and *Winter Numbers*, which was awarded both the Lambda Literary Award in Poetry and the Lenore Marshall Poetry Prize.

ACKNOWLEDGMENTS

Grateful acknowledgment is given to the following journals in which these translations first appeared:

Agni: Trees of Flame
Ambit (U.K.): Birds and Bison (sequence)
APR: Sacrificial Offerings; Solemn Vow
Barrow Street: Backwash
Chelsea: Appointment in June, Creation, Erosion, In the Square, Storm (I)
The Chicago Review: Moving Targets
Fence: On the Use of the Absent
Kestrel: Calendar, Gazebo, Refugee
The Manhattan Review: Furnishing the Islands, Harvest, Nativity, The Weight of the Day, The Wordless Woman
Meridian: Night Breeze
Modern Poetry in Translation (U.K.): Moons, Night Breeze, Storm (II), The Weight of the Day
New Letters: Almost Equinoctial, Mourning a Love, Sea Window
PN Review (U.K.) Storm (I)
Parnassus: Couples
Ploughshares: Hunting Season
Poetry: Alba, Pedestrian, Prehistoric
Poetry London (U.K.): Appointment in June, Gazebo, In the Square, Widower, The Wordless Woman
Prairie Schooner: Line, Reading the Branches, Widower
Shenandoah: Hoarding, The Holy Spittle, Rites
TriQuarterly: Highs and Lows, Horizon Line (under the title Frieze)
Verse: Facelifts, Gift, "Landscapes tossed away"

TABLE DES MATIERES

PREFACE DU TRADUCTEUR xv

HAUTS ET BAS 2

GRAVITÉS 18

"Le propriétaire de la villa..." 20
"L'arbre serre son poing mutilé..." 22
Arbre de flammes 24
Deuil d'un amour 26
De l'usage des absents 28
Préhistoire 30
Les poids du jour 32

LECTURE DE BRANCHES 34

"Blanchâtre comme l'aubier..." 36
"Par les jours blancs de la tempête..." 38
"Chaque fois que la voix déplie ses vrilles..." 40
"Comme si l'âme se défaisait fil à fil..." 42
"Dans l'oisiveté profonde..." 44
"Le jardin se replie sur ses sens..." 46
"Immatriculation..." 48
"La tête en bronze..." 50
Lunes 52
"Que la nature affirme sa changeante identité..." 54
Rendez-vous en juin 56
L'autre versant 58

TABLE OF CONTENTS

TRANSLATOR'S PREFACE   xv

HIGHS AND LOWS   3

GRAVITIES   19

Widower   21
Demolition   23
Trees of Flame   25
Mourning a Love   27
On the Use of the Absent   29
Prehistoric   31
The Weight of the Day   33

READING THE BRANCHES   35

Line   37
Storm   39
Wintering   41
"As if the soul unraveled thread by thread..."   43
"In profoundest idleness, when nothing..."   45
Reading the Branches   47
Calendar   49
Monument   51
Moons   53
In the Square   55
Appointment in June   57
The Far Slope   59

BISONS ET OISEAUX   60

"Cette rage sans larmes…"   62
"Des cris d'oiseaux tout près…"   64
"Ils eclosent à l'aube…"   66
"Rien ne dérange les canards…"   68
Rites   70
"Fourbu le bison…"   72
La très sainte bave   74
Couples   76

LIGNE D'HORIZON   78

HORS LES MURS   100

"Les mots vont et viennent…"   102
"Paysages jetés comme mouchoirs…"   104
Meubler les îles   106
"Plus réelle que la pierre du mur…"   108
"Inopinément les fenêtres s'ouvrent…"   110
"La trop sensible manucure…"   112
Belvédère   114
Fenetre sur mer   116
Orage   120
"Un signe?"…   122

LA FEMME SANS PAROLES   124

UNE LUMIÈRE PLUS NEUVE   140

"Échec et mat…"   142
"Roues géantes éparpillées…"   144
"On pourrait pleurer…"   146

BIRDS AND BISON   61

Hoarding   63
Matins   65
Moving Target   67
Hunting Season   69
Rites   71
Priesthood   73
The Holy Spittle   75
Couples   77

HORIZON LINE   79

BEYOND THE WALLS   101

Refugee   103
"Landscapes tossed away..."   105
Furnishing the Islands   107
Erosion   109
Night Breeze   111
Facelifts   113
Gazebo   115
Sea Window   117
Storm II   121
Sacrificial Offerings   123

THE WORDLESS WOMAN   125

A NEWER LIGHT   141

Checkmate   143
Harvest   145
"You could weep with these wintry tears..."   147

Ressac   148
"Craquement..."   150
"Ce bruit de talons..."   154
"Il y eut un hiver jaune..."   156
Creation   158
"Ô parturiente..."   160
Rêve d'exister   162
"C'est encore l'aube..."   164
Gaudebo   166
Vœu pieux   168

Backwash	149
Gift	151
Pedestrian	155
Almost Equinoctial	157
Creation	159
Nativity	161
Dream of Existence	163
Alba	165
Gaudebo	167
Solemn Vow	169

TRANSLATOR'S PREFACE

Claire Malroux was born in the Albigeois, in southwestern France, before World War II: the war and the Occupation, the death of her Résistant father and the survival of her family are perhaps the backdrop to all of her work. As a child, she left the south for Paris when her father was elected a deputy in the short-lived socialist Popular Front government of 1936. She completed her education at the prestigious École Normale Supérieure. She has remained in the capital, where she still lives, for most of her adult life, except for a post-war sojourn in England which led to her engagement with the English language and its poetry (her concentration until then having been on classical languages and the French canon). Though she had for years previously worked as a literary translator, and was already the author of two collections of poems, she describes as a signal event in her own literary life her discovery in 1983 of the poetry of Emily Dickinson , which she describes as "an encounter with the uncanny, " and the awakening of a "personal affinity." Malroux's ongoing project of translating Dickinson began then, and her own work evolved and developed along with it. She is the author, now, of eight books of poems—four published since 1998 .

It was through the poetry of Claire Malroux that I myself first became a translator. A poet since adolescence, an editor and teacher to earn my bread, and a student, reader and often quotidian speaker of the French language, I had nonetheless never made the leap from hearing the cadences of French poetry and prose in my mind while reading to transposing them into my mother tongue. I had experienced translation only as an adjunct to the process, by responding to French translator friends' and colleagues' questions—exchanges which made me vividly aware of the pitfalls, not to mention the embarrassment of riches, facing any translator of poetry.

I met Claire Malroux at a festival encounter of French and American poets, with Native American poetry as the guests of honor, in Grenoble, in late November of 1989—a festival which terminated with a Thanksgiving dinner for fifty in the town hall, with the mayor presiding, which may have given the Native American poets several layers of irony to cut into with their turkey.

As is usual at such festivals, there were readings every afternoon and evening. Many of the American poets present were already working with French translators, and made bilingual presentations. Fewer of the French poets had such alliances, and, since the Americans were, by and large, monoglot, this left the French poets' work outside the space of exchange the festival was meant to facilitate. I had been pressed into service as translator, oral and instantaneous, on several panels, which was probably what led Claire to ask me if I could, in haste, provide a rough translation of a new sequence she intended to read. The on-the-spot translation (done in a hotel room with no dictionaries!) served for the reading, but was far from true to the poem. But the poem itself, and the process of translation, had engaged me, and, back in Paris, I continued to work on it.

Perhaps if I had been more aware of Claire Malroux's own status as a translator, I would have had less temerity in rushing unprepared into her own text. It was in that same year, 1989, that she received the Prix Maurice-Edgar Coindreau for her collection of Emily Dickinson's poems published by Belin; six years later she would receive the Grand Prix National de la Traduction for her continuing work with Dickinson, but also for her brilliant renderings which introduced such contemporary masters as Derek Walcott to the French public. However, this also meant that the poet whom I was translating (the enterprise soon went beyond one sequence) was the most experienced mentor in the art one could imagine: quite apart from her own bilingualism, she knew as well as anyone what a translation could or could not reflect, in her own poems (and others') whether this were a question of rhythm, connotation, or even echoes of other texts which might or might not have resonance for readers in the receptor language. While we have never translated "à deux" in either direction, translation has produced an ongoing dialogue about language, poetic form, Baudelairean "correspondances," both in relation to Claire Malroux's poems and my own, but also to subsequent translations of other poets from and into both languages, by each of us.

As poets, coming from different traditions, we are very different from one another. Nonetheless, Claire Malroux's work has, as she implies here in her gracious acknowledgment and dedications,been subtly inflected by the Anglophone poets she has translated: among others, the Americans Emily Dickinson, Wallace Stevens and C.K. Williams, the West Indian Derek Walcott, the British Emily Brontë, the Yugoslavian-born Charles Simic, the Canadian/American Elizabeth Bishop. Her work has developed as well, of course, in dialogue with the French poets she most admires, including Jean Follain, Yves Bonnefoy and Mallarmé. She is one of those rare poets whose work is informed by day-to-day intimacy with a second language in its greatest variations and subtleties. With the striking exception of the poem-narrative *Soleil de jadis* , Malroux's poems might be said to be , in their own idiom, Dickinsonian, in their heightened, emotive landscapes, their metaphoric shorthand, and their familiar manner with mortality. But they are Dickinsonian often with the "significant absence" of the narrating / lyric "I". A bit of word-play that only works in English: the "I" in Malroux's poems is more often an "eye," observing, juxtaposing, concluding. The poems are neither autobiographical nor otherwise narrative: something which is not surprising to a French reader, but is more so to someone whose models for poetry are that of contemporary English. A narrative component of some sort is the norm for almost all Anglophone poetry , be it formalist, surrealist, "confessional," post-Beat, rap-inflected, regional or political. Even Imagist poetry hung on named myths, characters or landscapes. (There is, of course, the notable exception of the LANGUAGE poets who, not surprisingly, have aroused the interest of French writers and critics.)

Claire Malroux's own recent poems both distance and embrace narrative as the poet examines the texture of memory and of thought itself. Malroux's poems move between an intense but philosophical and abstract interiority and an acute engagement with the material world. The inevitabilities of time and change, the recuperative but potentially treacherous actions of memory, and the way thought is made concrete through the word are themes central to her work, whatever else is in view. Equally central is the poet's deliberate, sometimes daring work upon syntax itself, as the sentence is meticulously opened out to possibilities instead of contingencies, and played contrapuntally to the rhythm and breath established by the poem's lineation.

Malroux's lapidary earlier work drawing on landscape, seascape, and "inscape," was more elusive aphoristic than narrative. The above-mentioned intersection with the work of Anglophones like Walcott, Bishop and C.K. Williams may well have led to increasing reflection in her work upon the action of the agglomeration of events we call "history" on the interweavings of change, memory and words. "*L'histoire*" is a triple-barreled word in French, implying at once the macro-pattern of political and economic change, any sequence of events that occurs in fact or fiction (like your grandfather's childhood), and the story that begins "Once upon a time" (*Il y avait une fois...*) in the evening on a parent's knee or at a child's bedside.

The 1998 poem-narrative *Soleil de jadis*, (published in 2000 by Sheep Meadow with my translation as *A Long-Gone Sun*) is a book-length sequence which observes, through a child's eyes, the approach and the devastation of World War II in southwestern France, and the career of her Resistant schoolteacher father, an innovation both in the poet's own work and in contemporary French poetry in general. In it, "History" partakes of all those three meanings as the narrative metamorphoses from an incantatory evocation of awakening consciousness in a rural world to the gathering fragments of a bildungsroman of familial generations intersecting with self-discovery, fragments which are in turn exploded and dispersed by the arrival of something which seems external and implacable, but is implicated intimately in the protagonist's life: the war.

This present collection (of poems from the books *Suspens*, published in 2001, and *Ni si lointain*, published in 2004) also shows, but in a different register, an acknowledged cross-fertilization of Malroux's work by the themes and obsessions/ preoccupations of

Anglophone poetry (meditations which arise from memories and childhood recollections; the integration of myth with quotidian life; the idea of exile and displacement) as well as her attraction to a longer line and a often to a concrete, almost painterly setting which would not have been alien to Elizabeth Bishop. In Malroux's new work, also often more specifically urban in its focus, the strand of historical inquiry is elaborated in a contemporary context, while manipulating both metaphor and syntax with a deliberately disconcerting and innovative grace. In almost every poem, there is a characteristic and purposefully unsettling interpenetration of past and present which collapses distance and incarnates through metaphor.

After being awarded the Grand Prix National de la Traduction in 1995. Claire Malroux was named a Chevalier de la Légion d'Honneur in 2000 for the entirety of her work.

An idiosyncratic translator's note: the reader will notice that most of the French texts, apart from the sequences, are—like Emily Dickinson's poems—untitled, whereas I took the liberty of titling the individual poems, primarily to facilitate their submission to and publication in American and British literary magazines.

MARILYN HACKER
Paris, 2004

Le lecteur américain reconnaîtra au passage des noms ou des vers de poètes qui lui sont familiers: Emily Dickinson, Elizabeth Bishop, Derek Walcott et d'autres que je lui laisse le plaisir de découvrir. Ce livre marque ma rencontre avec ces écrivains que j'ai traduits. Ils m'ont ouvert des horizons, ont nourri ma réflexion et mon imaginaire, fortifié mon écriture. Je tiens à leur exprimer ma gratitude et à temoigner ici de l'amitié qui unit nos deux pays.

Claire Malroux

The American reader will recognize while reading the names of, or lines taken from familiar poets: Emily Dickinson, Elizabeth Bishop, Derek Walcott and others whose discovery I will leave to that reader's pleasure. This book marks my encounter with these writers, whom I have translated. They have widened my horizons, have nourished my thought and my imagination, and have enriched my own writing. I warmly acknowledge both my profound gratitude to them, and the friendship which links our two countries.

HAUTS ET BAS

HIGHS AND LOWS

Les heures tombent comme un rideau
à plis de statue debout
                ou gisant dans un sommeil
enlierré. On a abattu la forêt
couché les troncs dans leurs habits de tous les jours
mais l'homme sur le toit de son cerveau s'affaire
hissant les vergues de métal
L'aventure est à portée de fusée

La sirène peut bien se démener
dans son magasin d'antiquités aquatiques
courir de corail en corail
désenchantée elle se tait
rêve à l'empreinte de pieds sur le sable mouillé
                au soleil du monde
Le prince n'est pas encore mort au jour
bercé par les criailleries des oiseaux de mer
Elle ne mourra jamais à la nuit

Il neige sur les toits
Des pétales de lèpre brillent à la lune
sur les lèvres ensanglantées
Une nuit de neige tombe sans aube
                                un drap
les heures comme un rideau

January 30, evening

The hours drop like a pleated curtain
on a standing statue
                    or one stretched out in
an ivied slumber. They felled the forest
laid the tree-trunks out in their everyday clothes
but the man on the roof of his brain is busy
raising the metal yard–arms
The exploit is within rocket-range

Uselessly the mermaid thrashes
in her aquatic antique shop
dashes from coral to coral
all in silence, disillusioned
she dreams of footprints on wet sand in the world's sun
The prince is not yet dead to the day
rocked by the shrieking of seabirds
She will never be dead to the night

It's snowing on the rooftops
Leprous petals glitter at the moon
on bloodied lips
A snowy night drops dawnless
                    a sheet
hours like a curtain

31 janvier, matin

Rêvant
que monterait de la mer un lys pourpre géant
une pieuvre de feu
la terre ses diaprures avalées
comme un insecte cupide ou trop curieux

Dreaming

that a giant purple lily rises from the sea
a fiery octopus
the earth its iridescences devoured
like a greedy or too-curious insect

Sourd
         un grondement
                  monte de l'âme
sur la ville dormant
         (une autre s'éveille à mesure
         plus haut, plus bas)

Il suffit d'un insecte
         pour mettre en péril
                  le silence
mais souviens-toi
         qu'après le tumulte des alertes
un latin se perpétue en paix
                  dans les catacombes

Hymne de grillons
         soufflant leur musique
                  parmi les flocons

A muted
      rumbling
           rises from the soul
onto the sleeping city
      (and then another city awakens
      higher up, lower down)

It only takes an insect
      to endanger
           silence
but remember
      that after the sirens' commotion
latin will live on peacefully
      in the catacombs

A hymn of crickets
      breathing their music
           amidst the snowflakes

Parce que c'est lundi l'homme a repris sa besogne
il ôte une à une les écailles de son cerveau
Les parties noires se découvrent
Des moisissures frissonnent au jour
De vieux crimes mal lavés mal rasés se lèvent
étirent leur dos ankylosé
Des théories de songeries et de souvenirs
fuient par les interstices
Socs et plumes d'oie jonchent les décharges
Les oiseaux planent là-dessus avec dédain
qui pour franchir les mers
n'ont besoin que de renouveler leurs rémiges

Because it's Monday man takes up his tasks again
he pries the scales from his brain one by one
The dark parts are uncovered
Patches of mildew shiver in the daylight
Unwashed unshaven old crimes get up
stretch their numbed backs
Processions of daydreams and recollections
flee through the interstices
Ploughshares and goose-down litter the rubbish dump
Birds soar above it with disdain
they, to cross the sea
need only grow new wing-feathers

4 février, aube

Heure où le ciel vire de l'encre noire à la bleue
Qu'aurez-vous écrit sur la table où l'on coupe le pain
Quelle bribe trouvera le chemin
non vers l'oreille mais la bouche et le cœur?
Quelle saveur
plus inoubliable que l'ail et le miel?

même jour, tombée de la nuit

Pulsation s'éloignant en silence dans le ciel
son fanal
luciole, étoile filante, point nul à jamais
pour l'œil
aveuglément grand ouvert
sur l'éclat des balises à l'atterrissage

4 February at dawn

Hour when the sky turns from black ink to blue
What will you have written at the table where you cut your bread
What scrap will find its way
not toward the ear but toward the mouth the heart?
What flavor
stronger than garlic and honey?

the same day at nightfall

A pulse diminishing in the sky
its lantern
firefly, shooting star, perpetual zero
to the eye
blindly wide open
to the burst of signal–lights on landing

Danse de la pieuvre
notre aïeule   au fond des mers
                        Son œil de saphir
déchirant les voiles rouge sang
rond de ciel dans la chair préhensile
comme si l'innocence avait son paradis
à vingt mille lieues sous les hommes

qu'une autre création soit possible
échappant à la déchéance
sous le chatoiement

The octopus dances
our ancestor   in the sea's depths
                              Her sapphire eye
tearing the blood-red veils
a circle of sky in the prehensile flesh
as if innocence had its paradise
twenty thousand leagues under humankind

as if another creation were possible
escaping degradation
below the shimmering

12 février

Mer carnassière
dévoreuse dans l'inconscience joyeuse

Ne laisse pas le passé fondre aux rets du soleil

Irrigue de ta vigueur
les corps à peine nés

Et toi du futur
qui passeras ton rayon laser
sur l'archaïque écriture
par piété
ou souci d'exhaustivité
        N'oublie pas
que la main écrivait comme l'algue
fluctuante mais
intrépide alliée de la vague

February 12

Sea   carnivore
devourer in joyous recklessness

Don't allow the past to melt in the sun's nets

Bathe our barely-born bodies
in your force

And you from the future
passing your finger's laser
across the archaic script
out of some piety
or encyclopedic impulse
                Don't forget
that the hand wrote like algae
fluctuating but
intrepid ally of the waves

GRAVITÉS

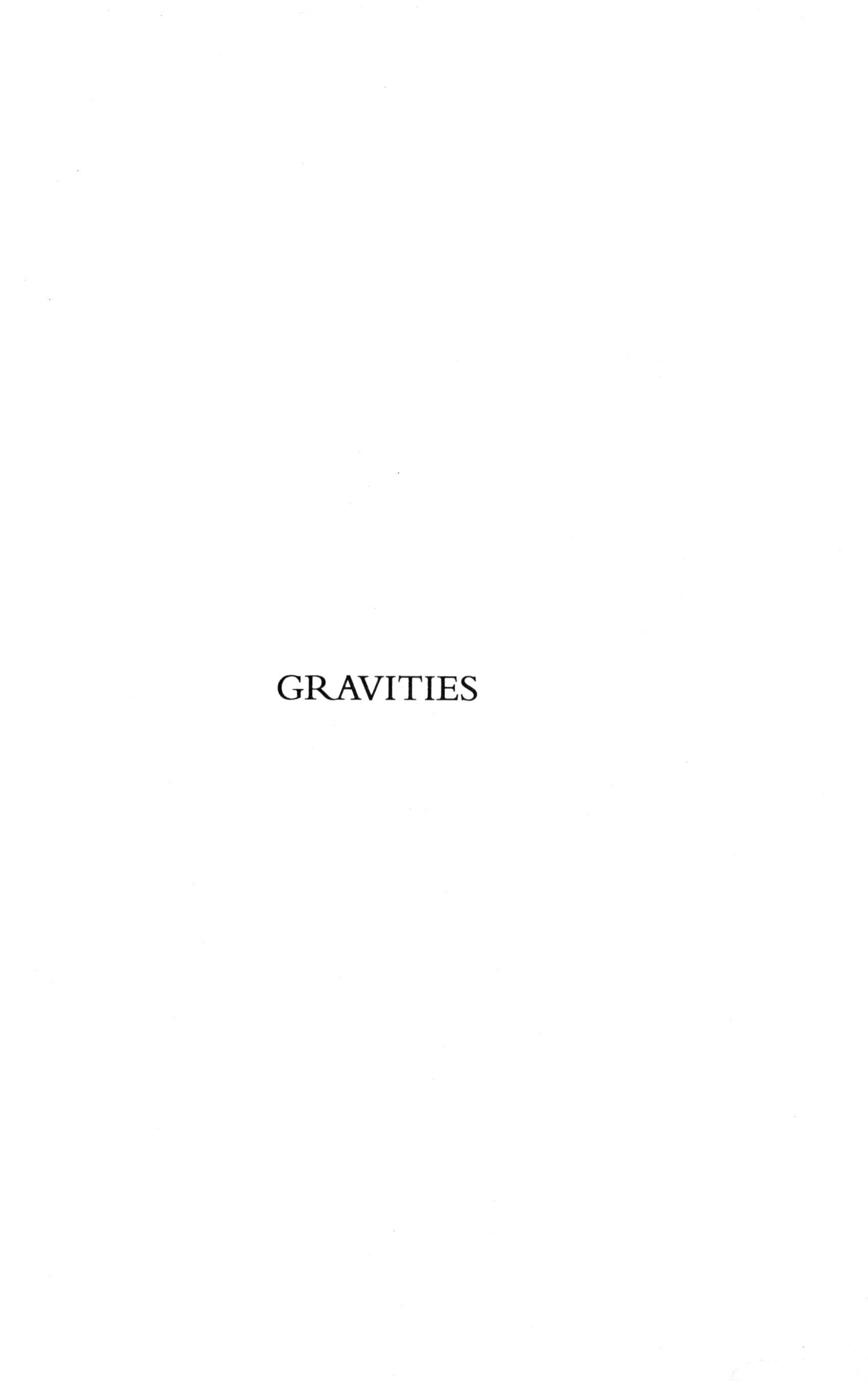

GRAVITIES

Le propriétaire de la villa dans son île
De verdure au milieu de la ville ne reçoit
Guère sous le cristal du lustre palatial
Écrasant la dalle d'une table. Il travaille
Sans désemparer, tout un niveau découpé
En bureaux fonctionnels, quoique au rez-
De-chaussée, derrière la haute verrière
Le salon déploie des tentures, des meubles
Rares et un piano à queue, lac d'où monte
Au soir un bourdonnement de rêves pour
Nourrir l'oubli du jour sans cesse à raviver
Le jardin étroit est pentu, un arbre unique
Trône en exil sur le gazon. La villa est
Bien trop vaste pour ce jardin, cet homme
Solitaire, veuf plusieurs fois. Mais de là
Il peut contempler son appartement de jadis
Qui craquait aux coutures comme un habit
De jeune époux, dans les jours débordants
De haine et d'amour, de désespoir et de vie.

WIDOWER

The villa's owner, on his verdant isle
In the city's center greets hardly any
Guests beneath the palatial crystal chandelier
Overshadowing a glass slab. He works
Incessantly; a whole level is divided
In functional cubicles, although, on the ground
Floor, behind the high French windows
The parlor spreads its draperies, rare furniture
And a grand piano, lake from which, each evening,
A buzzing swarm of dreams rises, to feed
The day's oblivion, which needs constant renewal.
The narrow garden slopes, a single tree
Reigns in exile on the lawn. The villa is
Much too vast for this garden, this solitary
Man, widowed many times. But from here
He can keep an eye on his old apartment
Which kept bursting at the seams like a young husband's
Suit, when the days overflowed
With hate and love, with despair, with life.

L'arbre serre son poing mutilé mais
Quand les cendres tournoieront dans l'air
Comme les flocons d'un hiver infini
Ses doigts se déplieront souples et guéris
La maison a fermé sa bouche ses paupières
De toute sa masse elle s'est rassise et pèse
Sur le vide retrouvé que de son amour
Le créateur avait cru anéantir
Derrière le fer et le bois, dans sa pitié froide
Le verre permettrait d'entrevoir, acompte
Versé par l'art pour chaque mortel,
Des larmes de couleur sur les murs pâles
Et sur le sol où l'ombre se déploie
Le reflet rassurant des choses caressées
Bêtes sans maître passant de main en main
Prostituées au corps de laine ou de soie
Tout revivra, un décor neuf chassant l'ancien
Des humains substitués à d'autres humains
Puis un jour une grue ou quelque guerre
Défera le catafalque, ornement d'une vie.

DEMOLITION

The tree clenches its mutilated fist but
When ashes spiral in the air
Like the flakes of an infinite winter
Its fingers will stretch out, supple and healed;
The house has closed its mouth its eyelids
It has seated itself with all its mass and weighs
On the reopened void which, out of love
The creator had thought to destroy.
Behind the iron and wood, in its cold pity
Glass would allow a glimpse, deposit
Paid by art for every mortal,
Colored tears on the pale walls
And on the floor where shadow unrolls
The reassuring reflection of caressed things
Unowned creatures passing from hand to hand
Prostitutes with silk or woolen bodies.
It will all live again, a new stage-set replacing the old one,
Humans substituted for other humans,
Then one day a wrecking-ball or some war
Will unmake the catafalque, a life's ornament.

ARBRES DE FLAMMES

pour Laure Bataillon

La mort cogne sur le miroir, éclats
Jetés sauvages à la figure du vivant
Mosaïque d'inhumaines superpositions
Sourire flottant au-dessus des yeux
Arête du nez comme un verrou vertical, regards
En hachures de pluie

Devant le geste suspendu, le verre et l'assiette
Jouent à colin-maillard, la table chancelle
Aucun baiser de sa buée ne fondra la glace
Du lavabo quotidien, même si l'ombre surgie du tain
À l'instant où tu crois faire rendre gorge à la nuit
Trouble ton visage, transgressant l'interdit
Elle vient s'éloigne à la vitesse de la lumière

Une explosion parmi les millions
De bombardements de la mémoire
Et tu t'inquiètes de connaître
Pourquoi elle semble être ton héritage
Ta part dans le testament d'une vie descellée
Comme si la mort était la seule porte, le seul alphabet —

Car des couloirs se creusent des carrefours se nouent
Dans les catacombes de la ville intérieure
Tout être croisé là est un sens qui prend feu
Sans ces arbres de flammes
Les images fracturées les intersections
Les inférences du monde supérieur
Ne seraient qu'arlequinade

TREES OF FLAME

for Laure Bataillon

Death knocks against the mirror, hurls
Brutal shards at the still-living face
Mosaic of inhuman juxtapositions
Smile afloat above the eyes
Bridge of the nose a vertical bolt, gazes
Crosshatched with rain

In front of the stalled gesture, glass and plate
Play blind-man's bluff, the table totters
No kiss's steam will melt the ice
On your daily washbasin, even if that shadow
Which springs out from behind the mirror, just when
You think you can force night to pay up
Disturbs your face, transgresses interdiction
It comes, departs at once, at the speed of light

An explosion amongst the million
Bombardments of memory
And you wonder uneasily
Why it seems to be your inheritance
Your share in an unsealed life's legacy
As if death were the one door, the only alphabet

For corridors are dug, crossroads are knotted
In the interior city's catacombs, where each
Encounter is a meaning which takes fire
Without these trees of flame
The fractured images, the intersections
The intrusions from that world up there
Would be a puppet-show

DEUIL D'UN AMOUR

en mémoire d'Emily Dickinson

Haillon de vent, l'ombre à la fenêtre:
Une vie d'un bloc retournée à l'oubli
Avec elle un pan d'une autre, car rien
Plus incoerciblement ne lie
Que ce qui fit une fois se croiser des chemins
À jamais divergents
De ces chemins seule la croix subsiste
Le silex presque abstrait de la croix
We met as sparks, diverging flints

*

Epuisée comme un soleil la douleur
S'éparpille en nuageuses vergetures
Cendres sur la voûte où la mémoire
Traque des conjonctions d'astres
Et doute à présent au bord du gouffre
Le témoin disparu, de la vérité de cette croix
Le livre est désécrit, plus blanc que la nuit
Miettes, rien que miettes d'écriture
Crumbs for birds, ces lendemains affamés
Piaillant à qui mieux mieux

MOURNING A LOVE
Emily Dickinson

Rag of wind, the shadow at the window
A life turned, in one movement, towards oblivion
With it, a fold of another life, for nothing
Connects more inextricably
Than that which made two forever-divergent
Paths cross once
Of those paths, only the cross remains
The almost-abstract flintstone of the cross
We met as sparks, diverging flints

*

Exhausted as a sun, grief
scatters in cloudy stretchmarks
Ash on the groined vault where memory
Tracks the conjunction of stars
And doubts now at the chasm's lip
With no witness, the truth of that cross
The book unwrites itself, whiter than night
Crumbs, nothing but crumbs of handwriting
Crumbs for birds, those starved tomorrows
Twittering as best they can

DE L'USAGE DES ABSENTS

pour C.K. Williams

Cette neige que les absents agitent
Sous le dôme de la mémoire
À des heures choisies par eux mais aussi par nous
Quand notre propre vie s'absente
On peut presque voir s'y imprimer leurs souffles
Et c'est comme s'ils chuchotaient
Qu'ils ne sont pas malheureux où ils sont
Mais ici dans cette serre où l'on s'obstine
À les greffer sur du vif
Quand toute fleur, disent-ils, toute chair
Doivent laisser le champ libre à la sève et au sang
Mais nous retenons ces yeux clairvoyants
Ces cheveux souples ces mains ces bouches
Comme si jamais il ne devait y avoir
De black-out définitif, notre vie
Suspendue à ce pouvoir de maintenir en vie
Et nous secouons nos réseaux, qu'en jaillissent
Encore et encore ces compagnons virtuels
Sinon les duveteux lapins et colombes
Et l'écran un jour se déchire
Pour que nous les touchions

ON THE USE OF THE ABSENT

for C.K. Williams

This snow ruffled by the departed
Beneath the dome of memory
At hours they choose, but which we also choose
When our own lives absent themselves
You can almost see their breath imprinted on it
And it's as if they whispered
That it's not where they are now that they're unhappy
But here in this greenhouse where we insist
On grafting them onto something alive
When every flower, they say, all flesh
Must leave the way clear for new sap, new blood
Still, we hold on to those clairvoyant eyes,
That flowing hair, those hands, those mouths
As if there never had to be
A final black-out, our own lives
Dependent on that power to keep alive
And we shake up our networks, so those virtual
Companions burst forth from them again and again
If not the downy rabbits and mourning-doves
And one day the screen tears open
So we can touch them

PRÉHISTOIRE

Un moutonnement venu d'un point infini
Roches grottes stridences d'argiles sous l'orage
Amalgames de goémons et de mousses brunâtres
Chaque marée pousse ses antennes de chair
Le poulpe persévérant se déploie, les crêtes
S'effondrent, tout cède au sable qui boit
En silence la sueur rouge acide et froide
Les enfants lancés à l'assaut sur la vague
Comment tourneraient-ils la tête
Vers ceux qui les ont portés jusque-là
Pour les porter à leur tour au-delà
Parmi la foule ils sont passés en riant
Ou pleurant sans laisser de mot de passe
Ils sont passés il court et court le furet
À peine si la mémoire ambulancière
Identifie les plus singuliers
Dont la chaleur remue en haut du cratère
Pourtant ils donnent à notre trajectoire
Sa rêveuse épaisseur: la chaîne entière
S'enroule dans la moindre de nos cellules
Et le temps d'une vie le temps s'annule

PREHISTORIC

Whitecaps surge in from some infinite distance
Rocks, grottoes, clay stridencies beneath the storm
Amalgams of sea-wrack and brownish moss
Each tide pushes forth its flesh-antennae
The persistent squid stretches its arms, wave-crests
Cave in, everything gives way to sand
Which silently drinks up the acid, cold red sweat
Those children launched in assault against the waves
How could they turn their heads
Back toward those who've brought them this far
To be taken even farther in their turn
They passed though the crowd, laughing
Or crying without telling the password
They've passed, the ferret runs and runs
Memory, the battlefield nurse, can barely
Triage the rarest ones
Whose heat shifts at the crater's edge
Yet they give our trajectory
Its dreamlike depth: the whole chain
Coils up in our smallest cells
And in a lifetime time annuls itself

LE POIDS DU JOUR

le poids du jour
                 glisse comme un
linge usé (ou même
pas) des épaules,

simplement frotté à la peau
les épaules
                 un peu plus voûtées
d'avoir porté un temps
une ombre de lumière

on entre dans la nuit
les souvenirs s'échouent
                    sur une rive
entre deux eaux
les étoiles flottent à l'envers

on ne sait pas si
on se reveillera ni où
quand les yeux des chouettes
se fermeront après la vigile
et le rat avalé

THE WEIGHT OF THE DAY

the weight of the day
                    slides like a shirt
soiled (or perhaps
not) from your shoulders,

simply rubbed against the skin
the shoulders
                    a bit more bent
from having carried
light's shadow for a while

you enter the night
memories run aground
                    on a bank
between two currents
the stars float upside down

you don't know if
you'll wake up or where
when the owl's eyes
close, the watch kept
and the rat eaten

LECTURE DE BRANCHES

READING THE BRANCHES

Blanchâtre comme l'aubier, à la base du cou
La ligne tourne sur elle-même, à chaque tour
S'enfonce et affleure d'un cran neuf
Cordelette de chair, auto-strangulation
Pli où dévisser l'urne précieuse, à ranger
Sur l'étagère avec les journaux lus, les confitures,
Les bulbes de l'hiver, les yeux de la statue
Dispersée au jour du grand nettoyage
Dans les décharges de l'univers, engrais
Pour les planètes sableuses, prenant racine
Loin du cercueil

LINE

Pale as sapwood, at the neck's base
The line turns on itself, and every turn
Deepens and displays another notch
Fine cord of flesh, self-strangulation
Fold where the precious urn will be unsealed, placed
On a cupboard shelf with old newspapers, jars of preserves,
Wintering bulbs, the eyes of the statue,
Scattered on the day of spring cleaning
In the universe's garbage-dumps, lime
For sandy planets, taking root
Far from the grave

Par les jours blancs de la tempête
Chemin et ciel couleur d'os
De hauts vaisseaux balancés immobiles
Ouvrant tout grands leurs flancs à l'ennemi
Le perfide musicien de Hamelin – celui-là même
Qui de sa flûte attira les jeunes feuilles
Hors de leur gluante maternelle prison
Dans son sillage les fleurs les fruits
Les merles les chants les prophéties
Les duos et les duels du soleil et de la lune
La caresse de la neige son boa d'oubli
Et la ronde d'enfants autour des mâts
S'enfonçant fascinée vers les racines
Échangés les aléas du sang ses creux
Ses flammes pour le halage du chant
Chemin et ciel couleur d'os
Par les jours blancs de la tempête

STORM

Through the white days of the storm
Bone-colored road, bone-colored sky
High vessels, swaying in place
With flanks open wide to the foe
The perfidious Piper – the same
One who drew young leaves out with his flute
From their seeping, motherly jail
In his wake, flowers and fruits,
Blackbirds, canticles, prophecies
Duets and duels of sun and moon
The snow's caress, fur of forgetfulness
And the children circling the masts
Plunging entranced toward the roots
Blood's risks, its hollows, its flames
Exchanged for the pull of that song
Bone-colored road, bone-colored sky
Through the white days of the storm

Chaque fois que la voix déplie ses vrilles
D'espoir, les lèvres de la neige
Volubiles comme celles des pleureuses
Murmurent la prière des morts
Ou la pluie abat sur le sol ses bouches
Voraces de nourrissons, dispersant le terreau
Tassé autour du plant par le jardinier amoureux
Jours d'hiver, jours de grande famine
Où le soleil est cloué sur son grabat
Et les vents piétinent son cadavre
Et les nuages passent en longs convois
Du soleil à l'agonie il ne faut pas
Attendre de miracles, mais attiser le feu
Rare couvant en soi dans chaque veine
Et souffler une rose, fût-elle de verre épais
Pour redonner vie à celui sans qui
Nous ne pouvons pas non plus vivre

WINTERING

Each time a voice uncurls its hopeful
Tendrils, the snow's lips
Voluble as a hired mourner's
Murmur a prayer for the dead
Or the rain dashes those voracious newborn
Mouths to the ground, scattering the compost
Heaped round the seedling by the loving gardener
Winter days, days of great famine
When the sun is nailed to its pallet
And winds trample its corpse
And clouds file by in a long convoy
Don't expect miracles from the dying
Sun, but stoke the rare
Flame smoldering in your own veins
And blow a rose, even out of thick glass
To give back life to whatever it is that we,
When we lack it, cannot live either

Comme si l'âme se défaisait fil à fil
Oubliés les éblouissements les éjaculations
Qui haussaient la sève et déchiraient l'écorce
Ne rien penser rêver oser ni désirer
Sinon la plénitude d'une nuit où planer
Dans le silence. Se changer en eau, en air
Dormir dans le roc comme le feu gelé
Garder la seule mémoire des mues de l'amour

As if the soul unraveled thread by thread
Forgotten the bedazzlements and ejaculations
Which brought the sap up and tore the bark
To think dream dare or desire nothing
Beyond the fullness of a night in which to glide
Through silence. To turn into water, air
To sleep within the rock like frozen fire
To keep only the memory of love's moultings

Dans l'oisiveté profonde, quand rien
Ne vient retrousser la moindre feuille
Et encore moins exhumer une tiédeur
Un espace découpe ses cavités
Négatif du globe plein qu'il réclame
La bouche tordue par une faim de nourrisson –
Comme l'arbre touche le vent à l'extrême
De ses branches avant d'être ébranlé
Il descend dans ce vide de lui-même
Aux marges où la langue se perd
Pour rassembler une espèce de souffle
Dont rien ne l'assure qu'il est sien ni
D'un autre à l'instant où il en est vivifié

In profoundest idleness, when nothing
Happens that could turn the smallest leaf
Still less unearth some warmth
A space cuts out its cavities
Negative image of the full globe it demands
With a mouth twisted in a newborn's hunger –
Just as a tree touches the wind with the tips
Of its branches before being shaken
He descends into his own emptiness
At the margins where language loses itself
To gather up a kind of breath
Which nothing assures him is either his own or
Another's, at the instant it brings him to life.

Le jardin se replie sur ses sens
Ni odeur ni bruit ni mouvement
Quand l'œil dans son vol d'automne
Tourne autour de l'acacia, sa couronne
De carapaces vides, papiers votifs,
Prières délavées –
Dépasse l'if à la raide robe tombale
Et choisit la gloire de l'arbuste sans nom:
Sept épées de feu, sept mille épées
De la douleur d'être ou de ne plus être
En migration vers la lumière. Brasier
Sur le promontoire de l'île
Il signale l'approche de l'ennemi
Plus intime à soi-même que soi
Et la mémoire alors perçoit
L'écho aveuglant des commencements

READING THE BRANCHES

The garden folds in on its senses
No odor, sound nor movement
When the eye in its autumn flight
Circles the acacia, its crown
Of empty carapaces, votive offerings,
Washed–out prayers –
Goes past the yew in its stiff shroud
And chooses the glory of a nameless bush:
Seven fiery swords, seven thousand swords
Of sorrow to be or to be no longer
Migrating toward the light. Signal-fire
On the island's promontory
It warns you of an enemy's approach
Who knows you better than you know yourself
And then memory glimpses
The blinding echo of beginnings

Immatriculation: samedi vingt-sept septembre
dix-neuf cent quatre-vingt-dix huit Jour d'automne
mais les feuillages sont verts et les oiseaux abusés
pépient comme au printemps Des marronniers
levant des cierges enterrent des rousseurs apoplectiques
Tourbillon des saisons   La vue se brouille
L'arbuste tend devant lui des bras de jeune fille
déjà vieille Ses cheveux ont coulé sur l'herbe
Peut-être y lit-il comme en du marc de café
et pleure-t-il toutes les lettres parties sans nom
ni adresse et qui lui parviendront trop tard, soit que
le soleil les ait calcinées de son excès d'amour
soit que les pluies aient léché l'encre trop pâle

CALENDAR

Registration: Saturday, the twenty-seventh of September
nineteen ninety-eight An autumn day
but the leaves are green and the deceived birds
chirp as if it were spring Chestnut trees
bearing candles bury apoplectic rednesses
Whirlwind of seasons Sight blurs over
A bush stretches out arms of a young girl
already aging Her hair has flowed onto the grass
Perhaps the bush is reading it like tea-leaves
and crying for all the letters mailed with no name
or address, which will arrive too late:
the sun will have charred them out of excessive love
or the rain licked them into illegible pallor

La tête en bronze deux arbres
La veillent   L'un bouclier d'ailes
Arque ses branches
Comme pour la protéger de la nuit
Ou de la neige   L'autre à genoux
Étale un lierre de roi mage

Trophée du jardinier endormi sous le gazon
Triomphe sur les feuilles
Mais c'est toujours la jungle
Pour le soleil   vieux singe
Sourd au carillon comme
Au glas de l'horloge

MONUMENT

The bronze head, two trees
Are watching over it One, a shield of wings
Curves its branches
As if to shelter it from night
Or snow   The other, kneeling
Rolls out a Magus' wealth of ivy

A trophy for the gardener asleep beneath the lawn
A victory over the leaves
But it's always jungle
To the sun   old ape
As deaf to noon bells as to
The clock's knell

LUNES

Pendant qu'arc-boutés sur nos racines
Nous vieillissions, les acacias ont
Envahi le ciel d'un jardin aquatique
Tout un réseau de rives s'auto-irriguant
Frémissantes, ardentes à palper l'inconnu
Nulle limite dirait-on à leur libido
(Sous les mousses de la forêt coule le torrent
Inaudible sinon pour nous de la naissance
Et dans les bosquets errent les troupes nues
Accomplissant leur cycle amoureux)
Élancement où les passions n'ont pas lieu
D'être et la pie jacasse comme un Dieu vain
Échancrures, lèvres sur lèvres s'écartant
Pour aspirer l'air maternel, jouir, bruire
(Considère ces vagues, feuilles aux yeux
Des aveugles mais tombant pour le poète
En lunes fertiles sur la fosse du ciel)

MOONS

While we, braced by our roots, grew old
The acacias had invaded
The sky of an aquatic garden
A whole network of riverbanks irrigating themselves
Trembling, eager to grope the unknown
No limit, it would seem, to their libido
(Beneath the forest's moss flows the torrent
Of birth, inaudible except to us
And naked flocks wander in the underbrush
Carrying out their amorous cycle)
A thrust in which passion has no
Place and the magpie chatters like a self-important God
Indentations, lips drawing away from lips
To breathe the maternal air, to climax, to murmur
(Consider these waves, leaves on a blind man's
Eyes, but for the poet, they are fertile
Moons falling into the trench of sky)

Que la nature affirme une changeante identité
Nous rassure. Le temps s'enroule sur le fuseau
D'une Parque unique, sans dévidoir ni ciseaux
Pourtant ces moineaux s'ébrouant dans la terre
Atomisée du square sont peut-être
Plus prudents que jadis, plus agressives les roses
Qui cernent les pelouses de leurs barbelés
Sous le masque forgé par les troubadours
Les instruments ont changé aux mains des spectres
Rassemblés dans le kiosque d'un autre siècle
Valses ni nobles ni lentes ni sentimentales
Le ciel semble fondre à l'appel des colombes
Mais durcit pour de futures glaciations
Seuls les enfants qui courent et s'aveuglent
De sable ont le même front en sueur
Les mêmes gestes les mêmes cris
Que ceux qui ici même se poursuivirent
Une vie plus tôt et les contemplent cloués
Sur leur banc tels de grands paons de nuit
Mais rien sinon dans leur ivresse de demi-dieux
N'est moins certain

IN THE SQUARE

That Nature affirms its mutability
Reassures us. Time rolls itself up onto the spindle
Of a single Fate, without a spool or shears
Still, those sparrows splashing in the atomized
Dust of the square are more prudent, perhaps,
Than they once were, and more aggressive roses
Surround the laws with their barbed wire
In a disguise forged by the troubadors.
The instruments have changed in spectral hands
Gathered in the kiosk a century old:
Waltzes not noble, slow or sentimental
The sky seems to melt under the call of doves
But hardens up for future glaciations
Only the children, running, blinding each other
With sand, have the same perspiring brows,
The same gestures, the same cries
As those who ran after each other here
A life ago, and contemplate them, pinned
To their benches like huge luna moths
Yet nothing, except in their godly drunkenness
Is less certain

RENDEZ-VOUS EN JUIN

pour Marilyn Hacker

L'arc des roses autour du gazon, leurs joues pâles
Laissant à peine sourdre l'angoisse du sang
Et derrière l'arc des roses l'arc des bancs, loges
D'où contempler leur candeur offerte au soleil
Glissant sur elles comme sur une page
Où bientôt les mots ne compteront plus
Le soleil grille les mots superflus
Qui le tiennent à distance, il brûle
En bon jardinier ce qu'il a fait s'épanouir
Ainsi tu fus en juin ma première morte
Le suc de ton cerveau emporté par l'abeille
Vers les rayons d'une ruche étoilée
Mon premier vrai poème peut-être
La chair tiédit les bancs mais nul vide
Ne flotte après le départ du couple enlacé
Les enfants jouent à prendre la petite maison
Rouge en haut de l'escalier jaune vif
Pendus à la rampe comme des vieillards
Une fille en brodequins croque une pomme
De son bourdonnement le trafic rassure
Y aura-t-il toujours des hommes pour embrasser
L'espace de leurs bras même bruyants?
Et de l'herbe, des roses pâles pour apaiser
Leur fuite en tumulte dans le néant?
Y aura-t-il toujours une figure penchée
Pour déchiffrer l'écriture du mystère
Bienveillant d'un matin d'été?
Quelqu'un quelque chose pour lui donner
Ailleurs un nouveau rendez-vous?

APPOINTMENT IN JUNE

Roses curve around the lawn, their pale cheeks
Barely letting the blood's anguish well up
And beyond the roses' curve, the curve of benches, loges
To contemplate their candor, offered to the sun
Which slides across them, as across a page
Whose words soon will no longer matter
The sun broils superfluous words
Which keep it at bay. Good gardener
It burns what it has first brought to bloom
And so my first death was your death in June
The nectar of your brain borne off by bees
Toward the rays of a starry hive
Perhaps you were my first real poem
Flesh warms the benches but no emptiness
Shimmers when the embracing couple leaves
Children play at capturing the small
Red house atop a bright yellow ladder
Hanging over its ramp like bent old men
A girl in laced boots bites into an apple
The drone of passing cars is comforting
Will there always be people to embrace
In the enclosure of their blood–loud arms?
And grass, pale roses to calm
Their clamorous flight into the void?
And will there always be a figure bent
Over decoding the benevolent
Mystery of a summer morning?
Someone something to suggest somewhere
A place to meet again?

L'AUTRE VERSANT

*"J'aperçois des gens, c'est comme si
c'était des arbres que je les vois marcher"*
— Évangile selon saint Marc

Identique est l'autre versant mais plus lisse
Sous le pied, comme si l'argile encore
Collée aux orteils émoussait la surface
Incliné pour former un lit ou un dais
Un pli de terrain retient la fraîcheur
Dans l'attente de l'eau, rivière vive, ovale
D'un lac nourri de neiges. Vallonnements
À l'infini, flous, peuplés de silhouettes
Comme dans ces images de livres pour enfants
En relief, avec des massifs derrière des massifs
Des troncs droits cachant d'autres troncs
Et des pousses minuscules, nains ou doigts
Germés sous les feuilles au temps des métamorphoses
Le château reste à découvrir, tout au fond
Un silence rouge absorbe les couleurs
Pour qui chemine à l'envers de la peau
Fuyant l'orage de pierre. Seul l'aveugle
Voit, guéri subitement de sa cécité

THE FAR SLOPE

*"And he looked up, and said,
I see men as trees, walking."*
— The Gospel according to St. Mark

Identical to this one, the far slope, but
Smoother underfoot, as if the clay which still
Stuck to your toes polished the surface.
Tilted to form a bed or a dais,
A fold of ground keeps its coolness
While waiting for water, living stream, oval
Of a snow-fed lake. Infinite
Undulations, hazy, peopled with silhouettes
Like those in children's book illustrations
In relief, with mountains behind mountains
Tree-trunks hiding other tree-trunks
And minuscule shoots, dwarves or fingers
Which sprout beneath the leaves in the season of metamorphoses.
The castle remains to be explored, there in the distance.
A red silence absorbs all other colors
For the person who walks in the skin's underside
Fleeing the storm of stone. Only the blind man
Sees, suddenly cured of his blindness.

BISONS ET OISEAUX

BIRDS AND BISON

Cette rage sans larmes dans l'automne
Quand la nature jette au visage le vin âcre
Et le miel de ses fruits et feuilles pêle-mêle
Comme une femme insolemment ses pulls
Mûris à la chaleur de ses seins
Et à l'acidité de ses aisselles:
Qui ne voudrait aveugler le monde ainsi
D'un kaléidoscope de moissons?
Mais balle, paille, épis pèsent sur la porte
Qu'ils empêchent de s'ouvrir vers soi — il eût fallu
Lier, botteler, battre à mesure — et se rapetisse
L'échelle pour accéder à ce lieu ouvert
Seulement aux hiboux où l'enfant qui dort
Enfoui là saurait tracer en se jouant
Une forme bien plus vaste que son cœur

HOARDING

That dry-eyed rage in autumn
When nature throws the acrid wine, the honey
Of her fruits and leaves, haphazard, in your face
Like a woman insolently flinging
Sweaters ripened in her breasts' warmth
And the acid of her armpits:
Who wouldn't wish to blind the world like that
With a kaleidoscope of harvests?
But straw, bales, spears of grain weigh on the door
Which they keep from opening toward you – you'd have had
To reap, thresh, bundle, tie in time – and the ladder
Shrinks itself down to reach a place open
Only to owls, where the child who sleeps
Tucked away there could scratch out, making a game of it,
A shape much more vast than his heart

Des cris d'oiseaux tout près, dans le lit
Même. L'angoisse n'en finit
Pas. Des boules d'une douceur poignante
Perçant le sommeil distendu. Il suffirait
D'étendre la main pour étrangler
Ces gorges comme d'un réveil la stridence
Signalant le retour des affaires du jour
Mais la main n'obéit plus. Est-ce une branche
Entrée par la fenêtre, avec ses brindilles
Qui égratignent et tous leurs occupants?
Cependant les cris deviennent des paroles
Incohérentes, cherchant un sens
À un drame dont le dormeur rêvant
Tout haut a perdu la clef, souvenir d'une autre
Geôle connue dans une vie prochaine

MATINS

Birds-cries so close by, right in
The bed. Inexhaustible
Anguish. Bubbles of a poignant sweetness
Penetrate slackened sleep. You'd only need
To stretch out your hand and strangle
Those throats like an alarm-clock's stridence
Signaling the daily round's return
But now your hand won't obey. Has a branch
Come in through the window with its scratchy
Twigs and all their inhabitants?
Meanwhile the cries become incoherent
Words searching out meaning
In a play to which the sleeper dreaming
Out loud has lost the key, recollection
Of one more prison known in a life to come

Ils éclosent à l'aube. Je les refoule
À l'abri de ma paupière, essaim labile
Une forme presque aussitôt disparaît
Parmi d'autres noires et rayées
Dans un puits au pied d'un immeuble
Une jette par la fenêtre un seau
Et des larmes roulent sur la chaussée
Une est penchée gravement vers la voix
Inaudible d'un gramophone à manivelle
Une autre relève un voile de cheveux
Et façonne comme un nid sur sa nuque
Avant d'entamer le rituel du jour
Déesse de la vie, vestale bien-aimée!
Sous les flèches du soleil je la
Fixe, la cloue au centre de ma soif
Émigrée d'une histoire sans paroles
Elle va peut-être ouvrir enfin la bouche
Me conter son voyage à vingt mille lieues
Sous ma mémoire, au pire
Me donner rendez-vous à un prochain épisode
Elle secoue la tête. Il y a dans la mienne
Trop de nuages, de neige, d'ornières, de vent

MOVING TARGETS

They hatch at dawn. I push them back
Into my eyelid's shelter, mutable swarm
One shape almost instantly disappears
Among others, black ones and striped ones,
In a well near the base of a building
One empties a bucket out the window
And tears roll out onto the road
One is gravely bent toward the inaudible
Voice of a hand-cranked phonograph
Another lifts her veil of hair
And twists it in a bird's nest at her nape
Before beginning the day's ritual
Goddess of life, beloved vestal!
Beneath the arrows of the sun, I
Fix her, nail her to the center of my thirst
Emigrant of a wordless history
Who will, perhaps, open her mouth at last
To tell me of her voyage, twenty thousand leagues
Under my memory, at least
Make an appointment for the next installment
She shakes her head. There are, in mine,
Too many clouds, snowbanks, potholes, winds

Rien ne dérange les canards sur la berge
Au soleil levant non plus qu'au crépuscule
Ni ceux dressés parmi la chevelure
Déployant sa rouille en constellations
À la surface de l'étang, étoiles tièdes
Pullulant dans l'hémisphère du froid
Le temps de même se multiplie, essaime
Dans l'immobile. Là-bas ils sont
Des millions à s'agiter dans les vagues
Et la frénésie de la danse. Ici tout est nu
Singulièrement, mortellement nu
Un plongeon, l'éclosion d'une bulle
L'épiphanie d'un être ailé
La présence adorée et haïe
Du chasseur embusqué entre ciel et eau
Qui par amour ou par jeu aura posé ses leurres

HUNTING SEASON

Nothing disturbs the ducks on the pond's edge
Either at sunrise or at dusk
Nor those others placed in the abundant hair
Which spreads its auburn rust in constellations
On the pond's surface, tepid stars
Swarming in the hemisphere of cold
Time breeds like this too, spreads out
Across the stillness. Elsewhere, millions
Flutter restlessly in the waves
And the dance's frenzy. Here, everything is nude
Totally, mortally nude
A dive, a bubble's hatching
The epiphany of a winged being
The adored and hated presence
Of the hunter in ambush between sky and water
Who's set his decoys out in sport or love

RITES

Jusqu'à la terrasse de la villa où le maître
(La maîtresse?) veille derrière ses pots de fleurs
Ses bols de fruits ses tartines en surplomb
Dans l'espace le gazon déploie un escalier
Comme une pyramide aztèque
Sans souci de hiérarchie les enfants singes
S'y pourchassent à l'ombre d'un Christ noir
Dont la tête ploie sous les épines
Vers le gouffre du monde ou de sa poitrine
On peut se demander s'il vaut mieux descendre
Vers la terre se rouler dans son lit plein d'odeurs
Monter vers le cou brisé pour l'enlacer
Tel le petit de la guenon de ses bras graciles
Ou embusqué avec les ancêtres l'arc à la main
Décocher sa flèche au cœur du temps
Pour entendre sa lente vibration d'arbre
Ému de sa blessure et nourrir de ce guet
L'énigme d'un bison mort et vivant

RITES

Right up to the terrace of the villa, whose master
(Or mistress) watches from behind the flower-pots
The bowls of fruit the stacks of buttered bread
The lawn extends a stairway into space
Like an Aztec pyramid
There, unranked in their play, monkey children
Chase each other in the shadow of a black Christ
Whose head bends under the thorns
Toward the chasm of the world, or of his breast
Would it be better, one might wonder, to come down
To the earth, roll in its odorous bed
Climb toward the broken neck to embrace it
Like the ape infant his dam, with delicate arms
Or, in ambush with the ancestors, bow in hand
Shoot an arrow into the heart of time
To hear its slow vibration, a tree moved
By its own wound, and nurture from that vigil
The riddle of a dead bison who still lives

Fourbu le bison non loin du geyser
De Yellowstone au sortir de l'hiver
Jusqu'à moins soixante degrés parfois
Mais rien ne fige la vapeur chaleureuse
Comme une haleine après la mort
Dans la bouche d'un cadavre
La vie étant peut-être ailleurs
Que dans l'évidence des signes
Déchiffre ce dessin au charbon
Par-delà l'eau-forte des miroirs
Intersectés de la terre et de l'eau
Ou d'une mémoire à l'ère sectaire
Du blanc et noir de la photo
Ignorant l'énigme en creux des grottes:
L'ambassadeur du vieil univers
Le moine au cilice de glace
Prisonnier fourbu des camps
De concentration de toutes
Les Silésies les Sibéries
A la volonté d'endurer
Embaumé dans la suprême
Majesté du Saint Suaire

PRIESTHOOD

By winter's end, the bison near the geyser
At Yellowstone is exhausted
Sometimes it's sixty below
But nothing freezes the hot steam
Like a breath left after death
In a corpse's mouth
Life being elsewhere, perhaps
Than in its material signs
Interpret this charcoal sketch
Beyond the etching of mirrors
Intersected by water and earth
Or a mind from the sectarian age
Of photographic black and white
Blind to the caverns' enigmatic grooves —
The ambassador of the old universe
The monk in a hair-shirt of ice
Exhausted inmate of the concentration
Camps of all the
Siberias and Silesias
Has the will to endure
Embalmed in the supreme
Majesty of the Holy Shroud

LA TRÈS SAINTE BAVE

Un rire, un gros soupir, a secoué l'horizon
Et quelque chose a jailli, des poussières de crachat
Au prisme d'arc-en-ciel, des fils
De laine emmêlés couleur de vieux nids
Ou de ces brebis que l'on voyait jadis
Non loin des tours de la capitale, serrées
À l'ombre d'un grand hêtre sur une île
Où des pommiers sauvages tordaient leurs bras
Mais on ne voulait plus de cette Arcadie-là
Les oiseaux tombaient en diamants
Cherchant au sol leur couronne
Le vent fouillait sous la robe de la mer: des poils
Clairsemés, des touffes blanchies; il en retira
Un amas de plumes grelottantes
Et une à une les effeuilla comme des marguerites
Ainsi la chair des choses se déchire
Sans os pour la retenir, mucus ou méduse
Empreinte d'une eau salie sur le sable

THE HOLY SPITTLE

A laugh, a heavy sigh shook the horizon
And something gushed out, a fine shower of spittle
Rainbow-prismed, threads
Of tangled wool the color of old birds' nests
Or of those ewes one used to see
Not far from the city skyline, huddled
In the shade of a huge beech, on an island
Where wild apple-trees twisted their gnarled arms.
But we'd had enough of that Arcadia
Birds dropped from the sky like diamonds
Looking for their tiaras in the dust
The wind groped under the sea's skirts: sparse
Curls, white tufts; it drew out
A heap of shivering feathers
And plucked them one by one like daisy-petals
This is how the flesh of things dissolves itself
With no retaining bones: mucus or jellyfish
Imprint of slimy water on the sand

COUPLES

Comme en haut d'une page
Ils attendent sous la tranche bleu pâle
Qu'un vent peut-être
Les cueille. Mais ils n'en ont pas besoin
Pour leur vol intérieur
Un instant les tente la pureté du vide
Avant que le soleil ne fore une ombre de jour
L'envie de froisser l'espace
À grands battements d'ailes inutiles
Par défi ou par jeu
Comme on se lance plus haut sinon plus loin
Sur une balançoire
La leur, cette escale où tout s'engendre
Et s'ils s'écartent l'un de l'autre
C'est pour aussitôt se rejoindre
Dans le cercle aimanté de l'amour
Mais sans cesser d'inspecter avec la même
Concentration frénétique
Les sillons de mousses de lichens
Riches en vermine

COUPLES

As if at the head of a page
They wait, under the pale blue slice
For some wind, perhaps
To gather them up. But it's not essential
To their interior flight
They're tempted, for an instant, by that pure void
Before the sun drills a false day
They'd like to rumple space
With a great beating of their useless wings
A dare, or a game
Like pushing up still higher, if not farther out
On a swing
Theirs, that port of call where all's conceived
And if they take their distance from each other
It's to come as quickly back together
In the marital magnetic field
While incessantly inspecting, with the same
Frenetic concentration
The furrows of moss and lichen
Luscious with bugs

LIGNE D'HORIZON

HORIZON LINE

1

En phrases
accouplées dans un climat stable
cocons déposés à l'abri des vagues
on voudrait que la vie déroule
une ligne d'horizon pure
et plate

C'est oublier l'abrupt des points
les fatigues des virgules
les espacements
et ces sautes de souffle qui cinglent
puis encalminent en alinéas
sans transitions possibles

Échoué sur
un de ces tertres de paroles transies
loin de l'arrière-pays
avec le trou noir de la mer
pour perspective

Il ne reste qu'à descendre
dans un tourbillon de molécules
pour disputer quelque forme à la mort
comme une fourmi
étourdie par l'avalanche de sable
sa boule de survie
arrimée sur son dos
remonte aveuglément

In connected
sentences set in a stable climate
cocoons laid out of the waves' way
is how we'd like life to unroll itself
a flat horizon-line
pristine

Forgetting the sheer plunge of periods
the weariness of commas
the blank spaces
and those swift breath-shifts blowing behind the waves
which becalm in indentations
with no likely transition

Stranded on
one of those mounds of chilled words
far from the hinterland
with the black hole of the sea
for sole perspective

There's no way out but descent
in a whirlwind of molecules
contending with death for some form
the way an ant
dazed in an avalanche of sand
its survival kit
fixed to its back
climbs blindly back upwards

2

Ne parle pas de noir
le noir est une couleur qui voit
matière intense et désirante
pointe d'un diamant
attirant vers la densité
de la profondeur

Parle plutôt de la transparence aveugle
de la glu du vide

Le trou serait un cube de murs blancs
une sphère de miroirs
où l'ombre tourne
et quête une goutte de sang
sur des reflets de nuages

Don't say black
black is a visionary color
intense and desiring substance
a diamond facet
attracting toward the density
of its depth

Cite blind transparency instead
the snare of emptiness

The hole would be a white-walled cube
a mirrored sphere
where a shadow twists
in search of a drop of blood
on the clouds' reflections

3

Où guetter l'explosion d'un soleil
en lieu et place de l'amour
cette main dérobée

Capable de découdre les paupières
dans la nuit des linceuls
de repeupler l'arbre
de feuilles aux lignes de vie
comme les siennes renouvelables

3

Where to watch for an exploding sun
instead of and in place of love
this absent hand

Which can unstitch eyelids
in the night of shrouds
repopulate the tree
with life-lined leaves
renewable like its own

4

Les yeux à peine clos dans la nuit
la plante boit la lumière
à nos yeux invisible

Sa pensée est sa patience
et patients l'air l'eau et le soleil
en leurs attouchements fulgurants
pour elle l'amour est temps non perçu
veine fondue dans le bloc d'ombre

Rien ne le différencie
des autres éléments
de la chimie de la vie

Moi, homme ou femme
j'exige
que le bleu sorte du gris
que le métal vil se change en or

Alchimiste malhabile
je dois fabriquer mon amour

Its eyes barely closed in the night
a plant drinks light
which our eyes can't see

Thought, for it, is its patience
and the air, water and sunlight are patient
in their lightning-flash touches
for the plant, love is unperceived time
vein melted into the block of shadow

Not distinguished
from the other elements
of life's chemistry

As for me, man or woman
I require
that blue emerge from gray
that base metal be transformed to gold

Awkward alchemist
I must brew my own love

5

Une boule suffit à obstruer l'horizon
façon de parler Ça bloque la salive
assèche le palais ligote la langue
On ne sait de quoi c'est fait le chagrin
on l'imagine rond sans circonférence
que l'on puisse apercevoir ni toucher
un labyrinthe courbe où tout ramène
au point lancinant de départ Ce feu
ce glacier cet acier cette soie
de l'amour sous tes dents mon amour

5

A sphere is enough to block the horizon
a manner of speaking It blocks the saliva
dries up the palate ties down the tongue
You don't know what grief is made of
conceive it round without circumference
that one could glimpse or touch
a curved labyrinth whose each arc brings
you back to the throbbing starting-point That fire
that ice that steel that silk
of love beneath your teeth my love

6

Sous la verrière
le soleil chauffe à blanc l'alambic
dans un après-midi mythique
de somnolence et d'ennui

Les jeux au bassin
s'érigent en rites

Transvaser l'eau fuyante
de forme en forme
tenir l'instant en suspens
comme une perle

Les moules se brisent
la soif demeure
d'être à nouveau apprenti sorcier
apprenti sourcier

D'étancher la blessure du temps
avec des lèvres d'enfant

La cicatrice se rouvre au jour naissant

On the glassed-in porch
sun brings the alembic to white-heat
in a mythic afternoon
of somnolence and boredom

Games around the washtub
become ceremonies

Decant the escaping water
from form to form
hold the instant suspended
like a pearl

Molds shatter
this thirst remains
once more to be a sorcerer's apprentice
apprentice diviner

To stanch time's wound
with a child's lips

The scar breaks open again at daybreak

Des prêtresses gravissent la colline
un livre sur leurs hanches
un livre sur leurs seins

En vue des Propylées
elles se troublent
le chant des cigales
vrille leur crâne
d'écritures de silence

Mauvaises apprenties Pythies
elles seront jetées en pâture
aux tigres repus d'Adonis
aux orties
d'un cimetière d'éléphants
entièrement incultes

Nulle cité ne s'érigera sur leurs dents

Priestesses climb the hill
a book on each one's hip
a book on each one's breast

Within sight of the temple portico
they become confused
the cicadas' song
drills their skulls
with handwritings of silence

Clumsy apprentice sybils
they'll be thrown at feeding time
to the portly tigers of Adonis
into the briars
of an uneducated
elephants' graveyard

No city will spring up from their teeth

8

Tapisserie de Pénélope
pétrifiée dans son attente
le cœur désert tandis que ses doigts
glissent comme sur un luth
aux cordes distendues

Rien que points à l'envers
pour remonter vers la tunique de noces
la brassière de l'enfance
repousser le point de non-retour
du non-retour de l'amour
égaré entre les bras des magiciennes
et les bras de la mer

Rien que la trame
le drame des jours sans drame
quand le soleil
fait à peine douter de la nuit
que le sommeil prend le corps
le jette au four de l'ombre
sur le charnier des survivants

La vie se divisant
tel un mauvais ongle

8

Penelope's tapestry
petrified as she waits
empty-hearted while her fingers
glide as on lute-strings
over slack fibers

Nothing but backstitching
toward the wedding tunic
the baby's romper
to delay the point of no return
unreturned love
strayed in sorceresses' arms
and the arms of the sea

Only the warp and woof
of untextured days
when the sun
hardly puts the night in question
when sleep seizes your body
to fling into the oven of shadows
into a survivors' mass grave

Life splits in two
like a bad fingernail

9

Les voiles de l'arbre claquent
se déchirent
embarcation toujours à quai
ce sont les saisons qui voyagent

Ce sont le soleil les airs
qui jettent sur les hampes
des couleurs d'étendards

L'arbre n'est qu'un mannequin
vêtu et dévêtu à volonté
un prototype de l'homme
tout en réseaux en organes
transformables ou échangeables
futur robot

La tempête un jeu
pour atteindre cet effet de véloce frisson
la course de milliards de roues
foulant le creux enfantin
de la paume de la négresse
Terre

9

The tree's sails flap
rip themselves
on the wharf always ready to get on board
it's the seasons that travel

It's the sun the breezes
raising bright pennant-colors
on flagpoles

The tree is just a mannequin
dressed and undressed at will
a prototype-human
network of interchangeable
nerves and organs
a future robot

And the storm is a game
to achieve that swift shuddering
the route of a billion wheels
trampling the childish lines
of her palm, black woman
Earth

10

Tombés dans le glacier
à bout de souffle
mes enfants que je n'ai pas connus

L'un passant un chamois sur la longue hanche d'acier
l'autre joignant puis écartant les mains
comme des moignons d'ailes
Se balançant sans planche
sous leurs pieds

Le visage qui les attendait
et qu'ils ne pouvaient attendre
seulement accessible
à l'instant où tout se fige

Brouillé sinon
et tremblant comme l'eau
sans autre forme que le toujours autre

Fallen breathless
into the glacier
my children whom I never knew

One passing a chamois-cloth over a long steel flank
the other clasping and wrenching apart two hands
like wing-stumps
Teetering with no plank
beneath their feet

The face that waited for them
for which they couldn't wait
only accessible
at the instant everything freezes

until then troubled
and trembling like water
with no form other than the always other

11

Même masquée de neige ou de grêle
la lumière avance

Les bivouacs de la nuit capitulent
spectres insomniaques
les phares s'allument sur les îles
pour guider son accostage

De fraternels signaux
s'échangent

Une à une elle ôte les housses
dans les maisons en deuil
replante le drapeau sur le faîte du toit
aux fenêtres de la libération

Prend place sous la plus haute porte
de l'arc triomphal

11

Even when masked with snow or hail
light advances

Night's bivouacs surrender
insomniac phantoms
lighthouses brighten on their islands
to guide it to the wharf

Fraternal signals
are exchanged

One by one, light whisks off the slipcovers
of houses in mourning
raises the flag again on the roof-peak
and in the liberated windows

Takes its place beneath the highest portal
of the triumphal arch

HORS LES MURS

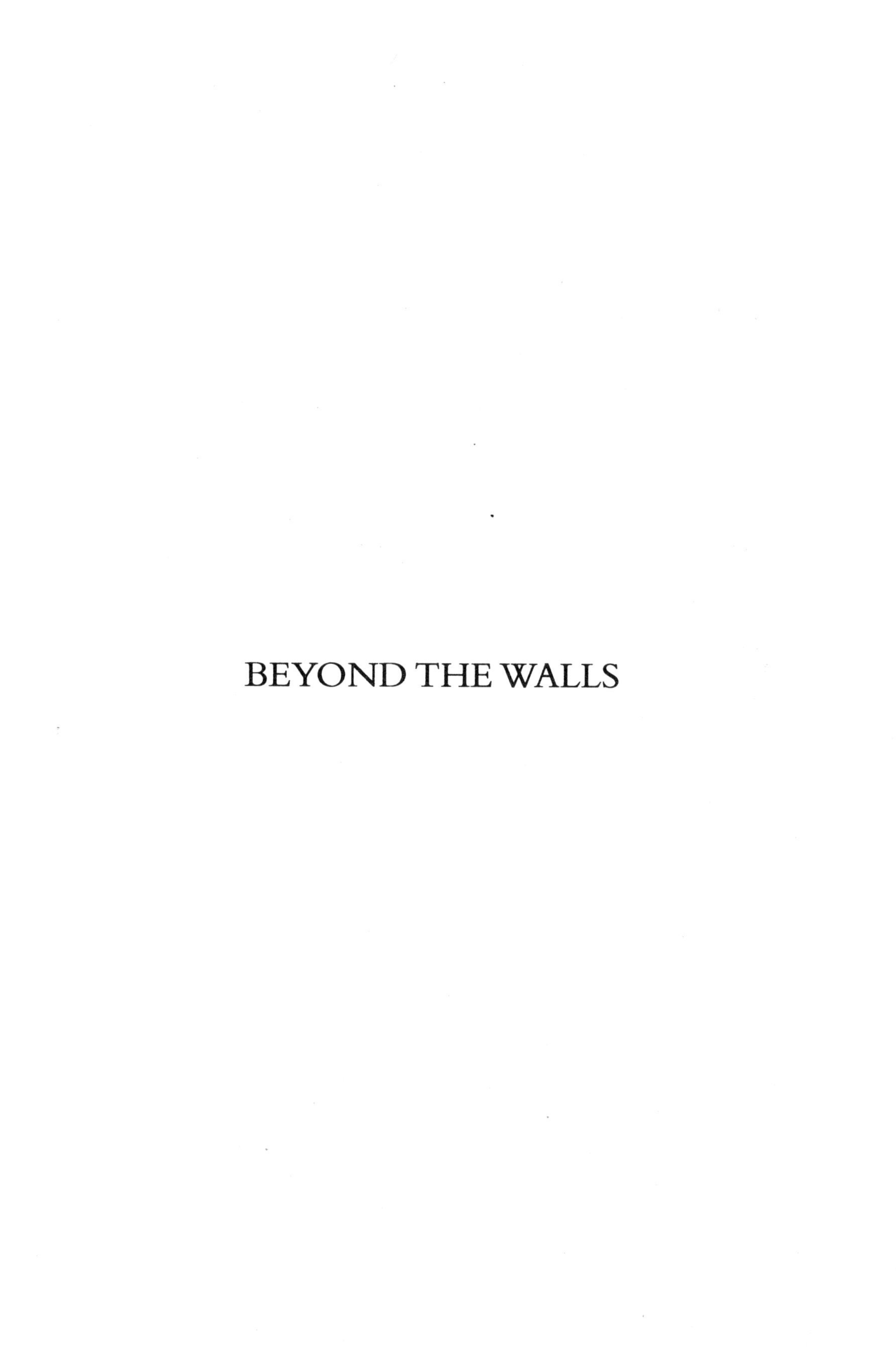

BEYOND THE WALLS

Les mots vont et viennent, traversent les mers
Ils volent vers la lampe blanche des corps
Agitant leurs banderoles d'amour et d'espoir mais
Ils s'épuisent se dispersent et la nuée de mouches
S'abat sur mon œil d'enfant qui fermente sous
Le soleil de Somalie puis le silence dans la luge
Où j'avais cru oublier la guerre, elle ronge
La cuisse trouée par l'obus semant ses fleurs de sang
Sur la neige de l'Europe incorrigible et voici
Qu'échappés de ces œufs de mort quelques–uns
Éclosent malgré tout de ma bouche et par des ondes
Plus subtiles que l'air vont poser au loin sur des paupières
Leurs battements d'ailes douloureux
Avant de fondre dans la flamme vers quoi
Les survivants de ce jour tendent leurs mains
Pendant qu'au verso de leurs fenêtres noires
Le blizzard vrille sa clameur et moi je tends avec eux
Ces mains sans chair sans poids

REFUGEE

for Charles Simic

Words come and go they cross oceans
They fly toward the white lantern of the body
Waving their banners of love and hope but
They wear themselves out disperse and the cloud of flies
Settles on this child's eye fermenting under
The Somalian sun then silence in the sleigh
Where I'd thought I could forget the war, it gnaws
At the thigh pierced by a shell sowing its flowers of blood
On the snows of incorrigible Europe and now
Escaped somehow from those death-eggs a few of them
Hatch from my mouth after all and on waves
More subtle than air alight on distant eyelids
With sorrowful wing-beats
Before melting into the flame towards which
This day's survivors stretch out their hands
While on the overleaf of their black windows
The blizzard drills its clamor and I extend with them
These fleshless weightless hands

Paysages jetés comme mouchoirs
De papier où rien ne s'imprime, à peine
Du bleu à lèvres sur l'épaule d'un édifice ancien
Une écume jaunâtre de larmes, des poussières
D'oiseaux chassés d'une falaise par la sirène
D'un bateau qui rentre ou s'éloigne et laisse
Perplexe sur le quai, d'un mouvement qui s'annule
Tous ces horizons, temples-jardins de Kyoto
Ou tells de la Syrie, énigmes proposées
Qu'il eût fallu scruter, mais sont-ils autre chose
Que les fragments d'une mosaïque au dessin
Enfoui sous les plantes adventices de l'histoire
Le scintillement d'une architecture de miroirs
Articulés pour capter l'incessant point de fuite
Quand la sagesse serait de bannir toute image
De s'enraciner pour la vie dans l'unique page
Comme l'arbre n'attend sa feuillaison que de son sang
Et du miracle métronomique des astres
Avec Iphigénie d'éveiller les vents et de bruire
Pour conduire au terme les voyageurs immobiles

Landscapes tossed away like crumpled
Tissues on which nothing is imprinted, the barest trace
Of blue lipstick on an ancient building's shoulder,
A yellow froth of tears, dust-clouds of birds
Chased from a cliff's edge by the siren
Of a boat which, approaching or departing, leaves you
On the dock, perplexed by its self-effacements.
All these horizons - Kyoto's temple-gardens,
Syrian ruin-mounds - suggested enigmas
We should have explored, but they are more
Than fragments of a mosaic whose design
Is buried under the casual weeds of history,
The sparkling of an edifice of mirrors
Hinged to capture the perpetual vanishing-point
When it might be wiser to banish every image
Take root for life on a single page
Like a tree which bursts into leaf from its own blood's signals
And the metronomic miracle of the stars
Rouse the winds with Iphigenia, and murmur
Immobile voyagers toward their journey's end.

MEUBLER LES ÎLES

Îles du temps, de notre *aire* de temps,
La quaternaire, où nous aurons fait escale
Dans l'attente de notre île dernière
Héritiers de havres clés en main
Sitôt émergés de la mer maternelle
Mangeant à la table des aïeux, dans leur faïence
Ou leur porcelaine, dormant entre leurs draps
Sous les images dont ils avaient meublé leur île
Et ces visages connus inconnus allumaient
Des feux de mémoire, creusaient sous la mer
Des galeries où nous jouions et rêvions
Dans l'oubli du naufrage lent de notre île

FURNISHING THE ISLANDS

Islands of time, of our eyrie in time
The quaternary, where we stopped over
While we waited to reach our final island
Heirs of harbors keys in hand
As soon as we're out of the maternal sea
Eating at the ancestors' table, from their earthenware
Or porcelain, sleeping between their sheets
Beneath the images with which they'd furnished their island
And those known unknown faces sparked
Flames of memory, dug out tunnels
Under the sea where we would play and dream
Forgetting the slow shipwreck of our island

Plus réelle que la pierre du mur
Évaporée dans le feu de l'été
Paraît l'ombre, promesse d'oasis
Durable pour le vivant aveuglé
Aussi quand tu perçois un déclic d'ailes
Un tocsin d'élytres annonçant la ruine
De pans de ton habitacle oubliés
Ne t'alarme pas. Révélation
Est leur écroulement. Il y avait donc là
Des blocs des tuiles et du mortier
Il y avait des sas des baies des vasistas
Pour communiquer avec l'espace
Et tout un paysage autour, des jungles
D'angoisses, des lacs d'amour, des haies
Dont chaque arbuste fut témoin d'amitiés
L'ogre temps n'en a fait qu'une bouchée
Se régalant de gravats jusqu'à la
Dernière miette. Et toi, que regrettes-
Tu, appuyé au chambranle qui reste
Seul debout?

EROSION

It seems solider than a stone wall
Evaporated in the fire of summer
This shadow, permanently promising
An oasis to the blinded survivor
So when you hear uprushing wings
Carapaces tolling the collapse
Of your retreat's abandoned beams
Don't be alarmed. Their demolition
Is a revelation. Yes, there were
Bricks, tiles and mortar
There were bay windows transoms pressure-chambers
Opening onto space
And beyond them a different country, jungles
Of anguish, lakes of love, hedges
Whose smallest shrub had witnessed friends' encounters
Time the ogre made a mouthful of it
Savoring the rubble down to the last
Crumb. And you, what do you regret
As you lean against the doorframe, all that's
Left standing?

Inopinément les fenêtres s'ouvrent
Tout grand dans la nuit Le rectangle
Engloutit la chambre c'est une autre nuit où
La vie comme un gant se retourne Il en
Sort une main veinée, feuille d'espoir
Négative sur la paroi fantôme
Pointant vers quoi? L'à-pic du lac
La neige des mers les lunaires soleils Il en
Sort une langue râpeuse mais tendre
Ignorant les garde-fous de la parole
Décollés les dessins les tableaux-miroirs
Les pattes de mouche du monde
Ils glissent des murs dociles et sans craindre
Le déchirement de leurs fibres
La lampe scintille dans leur sillage sa foi d'étoile
Les draps se nouent comme pour une évasion
Échangent l'étroite chaleur du corps
Pour la liberté des nuages douce et froide

NIGHT BREEZE

Unexpectedly the windows open
Wide during the night. The rectangle
Swallows the bedroom, it's a different night where
Life turns inside out like a glove. A veined hand
Emerges, leaf of a negative
Hope on the phantom wall
Pointing towards what? The cliff of a lake
Sea-snows, lunar suns. A rough but tender
Tongue darts from it, paying no attention
To the guard-rails of speech.
Come unstuck, drawings, framed mirrors
The scribblings of the world
Slip from the walls docile and unafraid
Their fibers will be ripped.
A lamp gleams its star's hope in their wake
The sheets knot themselves for an escape
Exchange close body heat
For the sweet cold freedom of clouds.

La trop sensible manucure du salon de coiffure
Un jour ne fut plus là pour tenir votre main
Une dépression grave. N'aurait-elle pas dû
En guise d'onguents passer plutôt ses nerfs
Sur les griffes de ses clientes ronronnant d'aise
Calées dans leurs fauteuils avec leur viatique
De magazines sentimentaux sur les genoux
Et jeter à leur face ravalée ses flacons de vernis?
Des immeubles s'effondrent d'un coup. Ou bien
D'une chiquenaude on les abat
(Ruineusement) comme châteaux de cartes
D'autres après une guerre lèvent un front grêlé
De mitraille ou ne peuvent plus fermer les paupières
En revanche, où penchait un garage borgne
Grimpe une paroi sans faille de verre et d'acier
Le cœur des villes est un temple qu'on rafistole
Au nom d'un bel hier enfui mais le sentier
Vivace, visage aigu dans le bleu d'avril
Renouvelle à l'automne ses sortilèges d'ermite
Qu'un rien émerveille. Refuge
De la joie. Celle qu'on croyait morte
Ouvre derrière les nuages ses yeux clairs
Pose hardiment le pied sur le sol après
Un somme léger comme les siècles
Ôte rides et verrues, balaie les rognures

FACELIFTS

The over-sensitive manicurist at the hairdresser's
Was no longer there one day to hold your hand.
Deep depression. Wouldn't she have done better
To use her nerves as salves
On her clients' claws as they purred lazily
Propped in their chairs with a provision
Of fashion magazines stacked on their knees
And fling her polish in their fresh-stripped faces?
Buildings founder at a blow. That, or
They're destroyed by the flip of a finger
(Ruinously) like a house of cards.
Others, after the war, raise bullet-pocked
Facades, whose eyelids can no longer close.
But there, where a one-eyed garage teetered
Climbs a flawless wall of glass and steel.
The city's heart is a makeshift temple
To a long-gone gorgeous yesterday
But the tenacious trail, knife-edged in April blue,
Renews its hermit's spells in fall – a hermit
Lost in wonder at a trifle. Shelter
Of joy. She whom you thought dead
Opens her bright eyes behind the clouds,
Plants her feet solidly on the ground
After a nap light as the centuries
Flings off wrinkles and warts, sweeps away the parings.

BELVÉDÈRE

C'est peut-être à cause de ce petit temple
Fragment là-haut de Grèce de basse-cour
Que je me suis vue me voyant ou plutôt
Nous voyant tous les quatre, minuscules, trois
Adultes et une enfant, la seule à la vraie
Échelle humaine, les autres feignant
De dépasser de leur taille et intellect
Les volatiles du lac avec qui l'enfant
Se sentait de plain-pied, et pendant qu'ils agitaient
Les noms de Lucrèce ou de Gadara
Ou se disaient que dans cette nature
Agencée à leur image d'êtres pensants
Ils étaient aussi bizarres que des statues
Qu'on exhiberait dans la forêt vierge
La fillette en extase comme saint François
Dialoguait avec les bêtes à bec et ailes
Qui pour l'heure l'emportaient au septième ciel

GAZEBO

Perhaps it was because of that little temple
A fragment up there of a hen-yard Greece
That I saw myself seeing myself or more precisely
Seeing all four of us, minuscule, three
Adults and a child, the only one who really had
The right human proportions, the others pretending
To exceed with their height and intellect
The waterfowl with whom the child
Felt herself on an equal footing, and while they bandied
The names of Lucretius or Gadara
Or told themselves that in this natural setting
Laid out in their image as thinking beings
They were as outrageous as statues
Displayed in a virgin forest
The little girl in ecstasy like Saint Francis
Talked with beaked and winged beasts
Who just then bore her up to seventh heaven

FENÊTRE SUR MER

Au fond de la chambre, des heures à
Remuer des éclats de nuit recouvrir
Découvrir ses traces (et vice-versa)
Traquer le pourquoi des zigzags
L'avancée nulle puisqu'on
Ne sait plus d'où on est parti ni quand
Explorateur dirait-on de l'extrême
Loin des caméras des ours des chamelles

Loin des caméras des ours des chamelles
En marche vers l'eau verte et les dattes
Haut levées des palmiers
Mirage de grappes de miel gelé
Sous le soleil vrillant... Il fallait fuir
Un poing (le sien ?) a poussé les volets
On a vu la mer immense fleur de soufre
Et là-bas on a hélé l'enfant

Et là-bas on a hélé l'enfant
Pour rafraîchir ses vagues mortes
Il tapait avec force sur le tambour du seau
Battait des mains même s'il sonnait creux
Au bout de la corde de son cerf-volant
Il faisait louvoyer le soleil
Les trombones d'or coulissants
Touchaient le feuillage de son cerveau

Ils touchaient le feuillage de son cerveau
De leur musique mouchetée
Là où les sorcières dansaient
Par les nuits de solstice
Mais la distance et l'oubli

SEA WINDOW

In the bedroom's depths you have hours to
Shift flashes of night to cover
Discover your tracks (and vice versa)
Map out the why of the zigzags
No forward motion because you
No longer know from where or when you departed
Explorer one might say of the extreme
Far from cameras bears and she-camels

Far from cameras bears and she-camels
Going towards the green water and the dates
High up amidst the palm fronds
Mirage of clustered grapes of frozen honey
Under the drilling sun...You had to flee
A fist (but whose?) pushed the shutters open
There was the sea, enormous sulfur flower
And down below you called a child

And down below you called a child
To cool down its dead waves
He was tapping briskly on the drum of his pail
Beating it with his hands even if it sounded hollow
At the end of his kite-string
He made the sun tack in the wind
The golden slide trombones
Touched the foliage of his brain

They touched the foliage of his brain
With their mottled music
There where witches used to dance
On solstice nights
But distance and forgetting

Dévorent les signaux qu'il renvoie
À travers les océans d'herbe du soir
Où la lampe n'escorte plus la lune

Aujourd'hui il s'écoule
Dans la rivière qui coulait en lui
Ses yeux sont de verre sa bouche éructe
Il s'éloigne vers nulle part
Comme un peintre
     s'absente
       dans le nuage
         qu'il trace

Devour the signals he sends back
Across the oceans of evening grass
Where now no lamp escorts the moon

Today he flows away
In the stream which flowed within him
His eyes are glass his mouth belches
He moves away towards nowhere
As a painter
                 absents himself
                          in the cloud
                                   he sketches

ORAGE

Un oiseau couleur d'avant l'aube, dressé
Mais flottant en fantôme au-dessus du vide
Dans le vide plus blanc de l'été, par-delà
Ce fleuve, cette ville pourtant familiers
Les wagons s'agrippant à la courbe comme
S'ils allaient se décrocher à l'instant
De buter sur les ruines d'une cité
Disparue, Resafa aux remparts de gypse
Les rails s'écartant entre deux points du temps
Ou de l'espace sans écartèlement sensible
L'au-delà étant l'ici perçu autrement
Croire aux signes dans l'angle mort
Où s'embusque hasard sans clef la poésie

STORM

A bird the color of almost-dawn poised
But floating spectrally above an emptiness
In the whiter emptiness of summer, beyond
This river, this city nonetheless familiar
The train-cars grip the curve as if
They would be uncoupled at the very moment
They ran into the ruins of a deserted
Town, Resafa with its gypsum ramparts
The tracks straying between two points in time
Or space with no visible distortion
The hereafter is the here-and-now seen differently
If you believe the omens in the blind spot
Where luck with no key, poetry lies in ambush

Un signe? ce cercle, une tête affleurant sur le trottoir
En son centre une étoile de détritus
Moins éloquente que l'étoile de David, marque
Jaune d'infamie mais flèche d'identité
Nulle dorure, rien que la pâleur du plastique:
Flacons de liquide pour la vaisselle, leurs vitres
Moirées par la pluie, cartons en bouillie,
Liens défaits, papiers gras, bourre de cheveux,
Ordures mises bout à bout par un fou de l'ordre
Ou de l'art comme des draps rêches mis à sécher
Dans un coin de la prairie non loin des toits rouges –
Humbles espèces offertes au ras du sol –
Au bassin de l'automne la foule des formes
Fouettées, repoussées contre la pierre
Par la loi du jet d'eau, l'épée verticale
Jaillie du bouclier qui est aussi la bouche aimante
Le souffle nous ôte du lieu de nos aspirations,
Mais des miettes d'espoir semées sur les marges
Pour les oiseaux, ensemble nous nous fortifions

SACRIFICIAL OFFERINGS

A sign? This circle, a head flush with the sidewalk,
At its center, a star made of garbage
Less eloquent than the six-pointed yellow star,
An infamy, but an identity.
Nothing is golden here, just plastic pallor:
Dish-detergent bottles, their slick panes
Silk-shot by the rain, cartons mashed to pulp,
Undone knots, waxed paper, wads of hair,
Trash placed just so by someone mad for order
Or art, like rough sheets hung out to dry
On a plot of prairie, not far from red roofs –
Humble currency, offered up on the ground –
In autumn's basin, clusters of whipped forms
Are pushed back against the stone by the edict
Of the water-jet, whose erect blade
Spouts from the shield, which is also a mouth that loves them.
Breath lifts us from the site of our aspirations
But together we can fortify ourselves
On crumbs of hope, scattered curbside for the birds

LA FEMME SANS PAROLES

THE WORDLESS WOMAN

1

La femme sans paroles contemple la pluie
Derrière le store baissé. Les feuilles
Bâillonnent les grilles, obstruent la gorge
Un couloir s'était ouvert tout à l'heure
Parmi le murmure pressé des gouttes, comme
Une foulée d'animal au creux de l'oreille
Les mots à présent battent en retraite
Replient leurs corolles La soie du ciel
Se déchire en un puzzle éclaté de flaques

Il faudrait tout reprendre à la lumière du premier jour
Ramasser ces éclats gelés sur l'asphalte
Réchauffer entre ses bras le dieu rompu
Osiris ou Orphée

1

The wordless woman contemplates the rain
Beyond her lowered blinds. Leaves
Choke up the railings, obstruct her throat
A while ago, a passage opened up
Amidst the raindrops' hurried murmur, like
A beast striding in spirals of the ear
Words at this moment beat a retreat
Furl up their corollas. The sky's silk
Tears into a puzzle broken up in pools

She must begin everything over in the first day's light
Gather those shards frozen on the asphalt
Warm in her arms the broken god
Osiris or Orpheus

2

La femme sans paroles, chaque musique la submerge
L'accent du pays natal l'obsède
L'ouïe la dévore
Lorsqu'elle se penche sur le puits de la voix
Qu'espère-t-elle remonter de ce noir
Où le caillou découpe des ondes de plus en plus lentes
Et plus sourdes?

Autour de ce no-man's land
Des forces sans étendards s'affrontent
Défaite ni victoire n'importent
Seulement la durée à franchir sans déshonneur

Elle ne sait pas de berceuse pour
Enjôler la douleur ni de rime en acier
Pour la dompter. Elle l'use comme un tapis
Un fauteuil où choit le corps las
Sous la lampe, un oreiller avec des auréoles
La mélancolie est son viager

2

The wordless woman is submerged in any music
The accent of her homeland obsesses her
Hearing devours her
When she bends over the voice's well
What does she hope to dredge up from that darkness
Where a pebble carves out waves that become slower
And more muted?

Around this no-man's land
Unbannered forces clash
Victory, defeat, are unimportant
Only a stretch of time to be crossed without dishonor

She knows no lullaby to
Cajole her grief, no steely rhyme
To tame it. She uses it like a carpet
An armchair into which her tired body drops
Under the lamplight, a stained pillow
Melancholy is her annuity

3

Voilé à l'angle du cimetière
Le temps attend qui ignore le deuil
Il est incapable de donner raison à tel ou tel
Événement et de conclure

La femme sans paroles répudie le sablier
Les mains émiettant le lézard arraché
À son sommeil de muraille Sa vie
Est une parole unique jamais achevée, à l'abri
Des phrases tronçonnées par l'alternance
Des jours et des nuits

Veiled at the corner of the cemetery
Time waits knowing nothing about mourning
It cannot fix the cause as this or that
Event and thus make a decision

The wordless woman disowns the hourglass
Hands crumbling the lizard snatched
From the wall of its sleep. Her life
Is a discourse never quite uttered, sheltered
From sentences chopped by the alternation
Of days and nights

4

Le jour s'efface devant la nuit
Comme un enfant
Que sa mère a laissé jouer
Avant de venir le border dans son lit
Elle lui conte des histoires
Qui nourriront ses rêves

Le soir tombé, la femme sans paroles
Refait le parcours des possibles
Hors de leurs rayons cireux
Des essaims de fantômes s'abattent sur elle

La nuit s'efface devant le jour
Comme une mère laisse l'enfant
Mettre à l'épreuve ses imaginations
Ses croyances naïves ses mythes

Day erases itself as night arrives
Like a child
Whose mother has let him play
Before coming to tuck him into bed
She tells him stories
Which will feed his dreams

When night has fallen, the wordless woman
Retraces paths of possibilities
Outside the waxy rays
Swarms of ghosts descend on her

Night erases itself as day arrives
Like a mother letting her child
Put his imaginings to the test
His naïve beliefs his myths

5

La femme sans paroles salue l'aube
Quand les nuages se noient dans le nuage
Plus vaste du ciel Derrière les tentures
Un prince s'apprête Il a tantôt le visage
Du soleil et tantôt celui de la mort
Avant lui les fenêtres s'éclairent: il y a
Cette lumière de l'homme ces yeux d'enfants
Au ras des bols leurs dents aiguës
Prêtes à mordre dans toutes les pommes
Tandis que sous les déserts d'étoiles
Les mouches fouillent dans les yeux grands ouverts
D'autres enfants absolument semblables
Et pondent les chapelets de leur espèce

The wordless woman hails the dawn
When clouds drown themselves in the vaster
Cloud of the sky. Behind the draperies
A prince prepares himself. Sometimes he has
The sun's face and sometimes the face of death
In his path windows brighten: there is
That human light those children's eyes
At the rims of their cups their sharp teeth
Ready to bite into every apple
While beneath deserts of stars
Flies burrow in the wide-open eyes
Of children just like these
Depositing their species' rosaries

6

Parler de tous ceux-là? La parole
Éloigne d'une mer où il faudrait se fondre
Pour ne pas se sentir recraché comme l'écume

Les vagues assiègent le pied de la tour
Par les lames de nouvelles meurtrières
Un nouveau Moyen Age s'annonce
Que les métaphores n'apprivoiseront pas
Plus de crépuscules ni d'aurores
Sur un globe assiégé de fourmis
Enchaînées à d'autres astres, rien
Qu'un clignement dans les filaments
De crânes fragiles et jetables
Où circulera la parole
Rechargeable

6

To speak of all of those? Speech
Distances us from the sea in which we must dissolve
So we won't feel ourselves spit out like froth

The waves besiege the tower's base
On the blinds' slats across our castles' loopholes
The new Dark Ages are announced
Which will not be tamed by metaphors
No more dusks or dawns
On a globe attacked by ants
Chained to other stars, nothing
But a blinking in the filaments
Of fragile disposable skulls
Through which rechargeable speech
Will circulate

7

La femme sans paroles appelle un verbe
À la consistance de fer et de plomb
Pour ressusciter la fulgurance de l'épée
L'art des rosaces
Un verbe tendre et fragile
Comme l'envers des paupières
Où renaisse l'enfance du monde

Dans l'orage du silence
Comme dans la jungle des bruits
Les jardins s'abolissent
Les forêts brûlent
Les semences se perdent

7

The wordless woman calls for a verb
With the consistency of iron and lead
To resurrect the sword's keenness
The art of rose-windows
A tender, fragile verb
Like the undersides of eyelids
Where the world's childhood could be reborn

In the storm of silence
As in the jungle of noise
Gardens are rubbed out
Forests burn
And the seed is lost

UNE LUMIÈRE PLUS NEUVE

A NEWER LIGHT

«Échec et mat» Ces mots comme un soupir
poussé par le sentier où la main d'ombre
paternelle ou dans un gant d'automate
vient de marquer un point décisif mais
la partie depuis si longtemps se joue
que nul n'ose hasarder de pronostic
sinon, ombre lui-même, le promeneur quand
sous ses semelles roulent les derniers pions
de lumière, débusquant un oiseau blanc, héron
peut-être, corps d'amante, mort ou sœur trahie
qui s'éloigne à sourds battements vers les étoiles
tandis que la tête noyée dans les citernes
les troupeaux achèvent de laper le jour

CHECKMATE

"Check, and mate." These words, like a sigh
the path exhales where a shadow hand
paternal or in an automaton's glove
has just made a decisive move but
the match has been going on for such a long time
that no one dares predict the outcome
if not, a shadow himself, the stroller when
beneath his soles roll the last pawns
of light, flushing a white bird, heron
perhaps, lover's body, dead, or betrayed sister
which flies off with muted flapping towards the stars
while, heads immersed in the cisterns
the flocks finish lapping up the day

Roues géantes éparpillées dans l'herbe
Chars de paille ruinés après une paisible bataille
Sans cris ni larmes ni blessés. Rien ne meurt ici
Sinon dans l'œil du témoin qui s'ouvre
Se ferme s'ouvre au gré du cycle des soleils –
Aveugle ou transcendant – c'est selon
Énigme d'une toile offerte à la frontière des saisons
Rouets d'herbe sous housses d'arcs-en-ciel
À remiser précieusement dans les greniers
Où luisent les contours d'une durée plus vraie
Parmi les maternelles armoires les tables
Les fauteuils les trictracs des comédies humaines
Accueille, mémoire, tout ce qui te désencombre
Laisse-toi traverser pour traverser les choses
Respire l'odeur du vide avant de t'y fondre

HARVEST

Giant wheels scattered in the grass
Straw tanks wrecked after a peaceful battle
With no cries, no tears, no one wounded. Nothing dies here
Except in the witness's eye which opens
Closes opens subject to the sun-cycles —
Blind or transcendent — as they pass
Enigma of a canvas offered up at the seasons' border
Grass spinning-wheels beneath rainbow dust-covers
To be stored away lovingly in attics
Where the contours of a truer span are glowing
Among maternal wardrobe-cupboards tables
Armchairs the board-games of human dramas
Welcome, memory, all that clears the way for you
Be permeable so that you can enter things
Breathe in the odor of the void before you drop into it

On pourrait pleurer avec ces larmes de l'hiver
Venues brouiller le visage du nouveau-né
Ses yeux encore clos sur son histoire aussi
Tragique que la nôtre en vérité ; vois, seule
Une fraction de ce qui est se retrouvera
Rassemblée sous le dais du ciel, seul constant
En ses mutations, tendu comme un toit
Sans épaisseur sinon des nuages parfois
Qui s'évaporent. Toi-même as vécu l'éternel
Retour de la joie, de la foi, de l'amour
Leurs cycles de plus en plus brefs s'espaçant
Tout s'est inscrit dans les sillons du cerveau
Mais nulle main ne peut dérouler, nul esprit
Pas même le tien, déchiffrer le parchemin
Qui durcit et se scelle comme une fleur sans pétales
Laisse le ciel pleurer, qu'il se mouille, se noie
Avant la brûlure du soleil la terreur glaciaire

You could weep with these wintry tears
Come to blur the face of the newborn
His eyes still closed on his history as
Tragic as ours, really; see, only
A fraction of what is will be gathered
Beneath the sky's canopy, the only thing constant
In its changing, stretched like a roof
With no thickness but sometimes that of clouds
Which disappear. You've lived through the eternal
Returns of joy of faith of love
Their briefer and briefer cycles farther apart
Everything is inscribed in the brain's grooves
But no hand can unroll, no mind,
Not even yours, decipher the parchment
Which hardens and seals itself like an unpetalled flower
Let the sky weep, let it soak itself, drown itself
Before the sun's burning the glacial terror

RESSAC

Là-bas on ne sait quoi se clôt, battement
De transparences sans traces de doigts
Sinon de sang pour guider vers l'essaim
Des bonheurs minuscules qui laissèrent
Un goût de lait et de miel
Chaque abeille
Éblouit la trame mais la détruit à mesure
Éveil d'un souffle caverneux sur la poitrine
De l'été comme en soulève la mer
Quand elle se jette contre le roc et le mord
Aux heures où la lune la flagelle
Byronesque suicidée
cherchant nue
Sous sa fourrure la volupté de la plaie
Encore une fois brûler ses lèvres
Au chaudron des douleurs, respirer le poison
Des entrailles en entrant dans la mort

BACKWASH

Something, we don't know what, is shutting off down there, a flut-
tering
Of transparencies with no trace of fingerprints
If not bloody ones leading toward the swarm
Of minuscule joys which left
A taste of milk and honey
                              Each bee
Dazzles the woven framework as it destroys it
A cavernous breath awakens in the chest
Of summer, like the ones the sea heaves
When she throws herself against the rock and bites it
During the hours when she's whipped by the moon
Byronesque suicide
                              feeling, naked under
Her fur, for her voluptuous wound
Burning her lips once more
On the cauldron of sorrows, inhaling the guts'
Poison while entering her death

1

Craquement, neige mate de la branche
Défaite par le vent d'une tempête amassée où?
Un coup de sang, boulets aveugles de l'orage
Sous le boutoir de l'air, la chair de l'iceberg
Ou les détonations en été à travers la maison qui se tasse
Salves de la vieillesse, écailles de la planète dessillées
Comme d'une tortue s'essayant à nager
Dans l'élément céleste

Le cerveau d'étoupe, si frileux (pour lui
Chaque fêlure est un gouffre)
Médite sur le hasard, la nécessité
Ne perçoit pas l'infime bourdonnement de l'étoile
Cachée dans un repli de son espace

2

Nous connaîtrons un jour des jours de plastique
Non biodégradables. En attendant :
Laper le lait de l'ombre dans le jardin en friche
Errer somptueusement sous la fourrure du chat
À l'affût de son double duveteux tapi sur les cailloux
Parmi les herbes folles. Un masque traqué par jeu
Ou le dernier avatar de l'angoisse
Avant que s'évapore la fraîcheur, que les yeux
À nouveau se brûlent au squelette

GIFT

> cadeau, *from* capitellus, *little head, iron tool*
> *with which armorers reamed out cannon-barrels*

1

A crackling, dull snow on a branch
Defeated by gale winds, which gathered where?
A blood-rush, blind storm-bullets.
Under the air's snout, the iceberg's bulk
Or summer's explosions in the settling house.
The salvoes of old age, the planet's scales unstuck
Like a turtle's shell, as it attempts to swim
In the stratosphere.

The kapok brain, shivering
(For it, each crack is a chasm)
Meditates on chance and necessity
Deaf to the near-imperceptible buzz
Of a star hidden in one of its crevices.

2

Our days, one of these days, will be non-bio-degradable
Plastic. Until then
Lap up shadow-milk in the overgrown garden
Sumptuously wander in a cat's pelt
Hidden from your furry double, crouched on pebbles
In the weeds. The ludic pageant of a hunt
Or the last avatar of anguish
Before the coolness dissipates, before your eyes
Once more burn to the bone

3

Tout lien de logique aboli par défaut de certitude
Un homme arpente les berges du fleuve
Traînant le filet de ses pensées
Poissons rauques à demi asphyxiés
Nul ne lui demande se dit-il de créer un vivier
Il s'agit seulement de survivre
Les peupliers tremblent, une haie de saules
Claque des dents. L'aile seule file droit vers son but
Le nid, l'œuf, la lignée d'autres becs
La merveilleusement vaine parole

All logic's links effaced for want of proof
A man surveys the river-banks
Trawling a net full of thoughts
Rough, half-asphyxiated fish
No one asked him, he tells himself, to start a hatchery
It's merely a question of survival
The poplars tremble, the grove of willows'
Teeth chatter. But the wings aim straight for their goal
The nest, the egg, the lineage of beaks
The marvelous irrelevant word

Ce bruit de talons sur le trottoir
Qui se rapproche   s'éloigne
Heurte le béton sans attendre la réponse
Parole errante   un pas menu de femme
Les semelles de l'homme
Annexant espace après espace
Froissement de roues sur l'asphalte
Cette Vespa lancée comme une guêpe

Loin sous la peau quelque chose se déplie
Racine sectionnée, vie qu'on croyait morte
Ou début d'un règne inouï, qui vient à l'air
Remplir le volume de l'air, ses pages
Ses interstices, un cartilage têtu
Un édredon de matière où rien ne résonne
Plus mais explose comme la mer mêle
Râle orgasme et vagissement, un cri
Dans un quartz de rires et de larmes

PEDESTRIAN

A click of heels on the pavement
It approaches   draws away
Strikes the cement without waiting for an answer
Wandering word   a woman's clipped steps
While a man's thick soles
Invade space after space
Whir of wheels on the asphalt
That Vespa takes off like a wasp...

Far below the surface, something unfolds
Severed root, life you thought extinguished
Or start of an unprecedented reign
Which comes to fill the volume of the air,
Its pages, its interstices: tough cartilage,
Quilt of stuff through which nothing resonates,
Explodes, instead, the way the sea
Blends death-rattle, orgasm, birth-wail, a cry
Within a crystal of tears and laughter

Il y eut un hiver jaune, sans même le néon de la neige
Un brouillard d'iceberg, la ville recluse dans sa pierre
Si vieille tout à coup, ôtées la volubilité des feuilles
Sur un mur et les voix flâneuses dans les ruelles
L'histoire allait son train ailleurs, là où la neige
Allumait un fanal au feu du sang. On pensait tunnel
Couloir d'hôpital emballage à la Christo pierre
Et humains liés en une larve monumentale
On pensait eaux troubles d'avant le corps, ocre
De la poussière originelle exode cancers et sidas
Sous le drap du ciel. Pourtant une stridence
Trouait cette ouate, comme d'un sourd s'obstinant
À lancer à tue-tête son cantique de grillon
Aux étoiles fantômes et d'on ne sait où
Filtra le jour d'une lumière plus neuve

ALMOST EQUINOCTIAL

There was once a yellow winter, without even the neon of snow
An iceberg of fog, the city withdrew in its stone
Suddenly so old, with the voluble leaves on a wall,
The strolling voices in sidestreets lifted away
History carried on elsewhere, there where the snow
Lit up a bloody lantern. One thought: tunnel,
Hospital corridor, Christo's wrappings, stone
And humans bound in a monumental cocoon
One thought: murky amniotic water, ochre
Of the first dust, exodus, cancers and AIDS
Beneath the sheet of sky. And yet a stridency
Tore through that cotton-wool, as if a deaf man insisted
On shouting his cricket's canticle at the top of his lungs
Toward the phantom stars and there filtered in from who
Knows where, a day with newer light.

CRÉATION

Bleu d'une mer étalé sur les toits et sans écume
À jamais. L'air tendu comme la soie d'un parapluie
Empêche que l'on s'y jette, que l'on s'y noie
Même les oiseaux n'osent ébouriffer leurs plumes
Certaines aubes se déchirent en fibres de mensonge
Ou en placentas stériles, mais celle-ci glisse
Comme huilée de la nuit du vagin. Expertes
Les mains de la lumière haussent l'offrande
La volonté de l'homme l'imite dans son sommeil
Appliquant une à une ses feuilles d'or
Sur la coupole de l'édifice intérieur
Chaumière, palais, temple ou bordel

CREATION

The simple, naked sky
Is it rich, then?
— Hölderlin

Sea-blue spread across the roofs, foamless
Forever. Air stretched silk-taut in umbrella-ribs
Keeps us from diving in, from drowning there.
Even the birds don't dare ruffle their feathers.
Certain dawns shred themselves in ragged lies
Or sterile afterbirths, but this one slips
Slick from vaginal night. The expert hands
Of light raise up the offering.
Our human will mimes the motion in sleep,
Laying down gold leaves one by one on this
Dome of an interior edifice
Thatched hut, palace, temple, or brothel.

Ô parturiente, de qui l'enfant enlaçant
De ses bras clairs le phare là-bas qui désigne
Le feu, comme sur nos colonnes l'amour à cheval
S'illumine et s'envole dans l'espace
Purgé du tumulte des nuages? L'éclair de la nuit
Frappe les maisons aveugles du quai, leurs oreilles
Tournées vers la pluie d'or, leurs bouches avares
Sous la lune la mer balbutie des sagas de vagues
Toujours il a manqué un souffle plus ailé
Un battement plus vif ou plus lent, et l'ombre
Visiteuse s'est fondue dans l'armée des muets.
Le ciel dénudant son thorax ne montre ni cœur
Ni poumons ni plaie non plus sous ses côtes
Fines comme des veines. Vite le soleil
S'applique à sécher les larmes larves incolores
C'est à cet instant de l'inconcevable, à cet instant
De mort, qu'un corps choisit de naître

NATIVITY

O Parturient, whose is this child encircling
With bright arms the lighthouse there which signals
Fire, as atop our columns love on horseback
Is lit up and takes off into space
Purged of the tumult of clouds? The night-beam
Strikes the blind houses on the wharf, their ears
And avid mouths turned toward the golden rain.
Beneath the moon, the sea stammers sagas of waves.
Something has always been missing – a more winged breath
A quicker or slower beat, and the visiting
Shadow has melted into the mute throng.
The sky baring its torso shows neither heart
Nor lungs nor wound beneath its ribs
As fine as veins. Quickly the sun
Busies itself drying up those colorless larval tears
It's at that instant of the inconceivable, that instant
Of death, that a body chooses to be born

RÊVE D'EXISTER

Il a surgi à l'angle de ma rue
Nouveau-né plusieurs fois séculaire
S'est bercé un temps dans son hamac
Entre deux géométriques falaises
Admirant la densité de la cité
Frimousse d'ange aussi lisse
Que la bleue solitude d'un lac
Lui-même d'une fraîcheur de neige
Mais avant la nuit s'est éclipsé
Ayant croisé un rayon meurtrier
Ou le regard d'une ombre en bas
Et fuyant d'instinct le chemin
Des larmes souterraines

DREAM OF EXISTENCE

It appeared on my street corner
Newborn, infinitely secular
Rocked itself awhile in its hammock
Between two geometric cliffs
Admiring the urban density
Cherubic face as sleek
As the blue solitude of a lake
And as cool itself as fresh snow
But slipped away before nightfall
Having met up with a lethal ray
Or the gaze of a shadow below
And instinctively fleeing the path
Of subterranean tears

C'est encore l'aube et c'est encore l'aube
Et c'est encore l'aube, arc vers quoi la cible
Se tend, œil oublieux de sa chambre obscure
Théâtre où de lignes couleurs reliefs resurgit
Sous la régie solaire loin en surface
Infailliblement un temps combien le décor

C'est encore l'aube et c'est encore l'aube
Avec les rires des mésanges les anges
Qui se piquent les doigts en riant aux voiles
Païens de leur sœur et la sphère vole
Sous ses chiffons de nerfs et de sang
Avec tous les oiseaux qui frôlent les mers
Et sur nos mâts posent leurs ailes du même mauve
Avant de franchir d'autres mers Jamais longtemps
Les mêmes yeux pour suivre leur exode

C'est encore l'aube et la grâce
D'être comparse de l'acte de magie
Joué des trillions de fois trillions de trilles
Mais guère plus de trente mille pour l'humain
Dont les chiffres bornent le cerveau C'est
Encore l'aube le braille sous les doigts
Mouillés par la semence et c'est encore
L'aube et c'est encore l'aube

ALBA

It's dawn again and once again it's dawn
And it's dawn again, drawn bow toward which the target
Tightens, eye forgetting its darkroom
Theater where from lines colors textures reemerges
Under the sun's direction, deceptively distant,
Unfailingly for a while, how long, this stage-set

It's dawn again and once again it's dawn
With the laughter of oriole angels
Who prick their fingers mocking their sister's
Pagan veils and the sphere flies
In its rags of nerve and blood
With all the birds who skim the seas
And fold their wings on our masts, mauve upon mauve
Before breasting other seas. Never for long
Do the same eyes follow their exodus

It's dawn again and the grace
Of being an extra in this magic show
Played out trillions of times, trillions of trills
But hardly more than thirty thousand for humans
Whose figures bind their brains. It's
Dawn again, braille beneath fingers
Moist with sperm and it's dawn
Again and once again it's dawn

GAUDEBO

pour Derek Walcott

Gaudebo – parole soufflée en rêve
Dans *le merveilleux latin* qui perdure
Quoique *perdu pour toutes nos écoles*
Allons nous réjouir sur l'autel du Seigneur
Chante Racine ou un ancien catéchisme
Gaudebo pour cet enfant en sabots
Avançant sur la plaine où le vent pousse
La neige buissonnière sans alphabet
Sinon les bosses du monde et ses plaies
Gaudebo car descendant l'allée du jardin
Dans les siècles des siècles de juin
Il recevait le sacrement de l'aube;
La nuit dans le seul globe de son œil
Ramenait les étoiles, cœurs glacés
Mais palpitants, et embrassant les saisons
La rivière parlait en voyelles frottées
Contre le rauque ivoire des rochers
Que de temps s'est écoulé pour que la gorge
Brûlée obstruée de cailloux se délie!
Presque autant que pour déboucher sur la lande
Nue de la mort après les péripéties
Mais parce que sans faillir le gargouillis
Comme d'un sexe doucement mouillé
Monte des racines vers l'autel de l'inutile
Gaudebo

GAUDEBO

for Derek Walcott

Gaudebo – word breathed out in a dream
In the *lovely Latin* which survives
Although *lost to all of our schools*
Let us rejoice at the Lord's altar
Intone Racine or an old catechism
Gaudebo for that child in wooden clogs
Coming across the plain where the wind sweeps
The truant snow whose only alphabet
Is the planet's bruises and wounds
Gaudebo for on the garden path
In the world without end of June
He received the sacrament of dawn;
For the sole orbit of his eyes, the night
Gathered up stars, frozen but
Beating hearts, and, embracing the seasons
The river spoke in vowels rubbed raw against
The raucous ivory of the rocks
How much time had to pass for that scorched
Throat blocked with stones to break loose!
As much as it took to emerge on the nude
Moor of death after so much wandering
But because a sound unfailingly froths up
Like a woman's gently moistened sex
From the roots to the altar of idleness
Gaudebo

VŒU PIEUX

Casser les mots comme on fend le silex
Broyer les mots comme le marbre ou les couleurs
Que monte la poussière aux narines du dieu
Fine comme le blé moulu pour le pain de tous
Comme la poudre sur les joues des femmes belles
Et moins belles, le pollen des papillons, le sel
Des embruns perçant les portes de la mer
Comme l'air où palpitent des milliards d'ampoules
Comme le grain du temps éclaté dans le sablier
Libérer les atomes de la parole avant
Que les mots ne cassent, ne broient,
Ne calcinent, ne dispersent, n'ensevelissent

SOLEMN VOW

I will break words up the way I'd split a flint
I will grind words down like marble, like pigments
So their dust rises to the nostrils of the god
Fine-ground as flour for our daily bread
Or powder on the cheeks of beautiful
And less beautiful women, butterflies' pollen, salt
Of the spindrift piercing the doors of the sea
Like the air where a billion light bulbs palpitate
Like the grain of time burst in the hourglass
I will set free those atoms of speech before
Words themselves break me up, grind me down,
Burn me to ash, scatter me, bury me